KW-222-564

Contents

"WE CONSIDER that specific provision for direct moral instruction in the school programme is highly desirable ... one or two periods a week should be set aside in the school timetable for instruction in moral and spiritual values ... At the secondary stage there may be frequent discussions between teacher and the pupils on the values sought to be inculcated. Whatever be the method of teaching, it should not lead to moral instruction being divorced from the rest of the curriculum or being confined to a single period. If values are to become part of the students' character, an all-embracing treatment of the moral way of life is needed."

KOTHARI REPORT

"I WANT INDIA to have schools and colleges where the aim of the teachers is to produce unselfish, fearless and faith-filled men and women. Not the general desire, mind you, but the steady aim in all they do or don't do. And I want to see students who are more concerned about the training they get to serve their fellow men and less about a certificate that will bring within their reach a career or fame. ...

"Where students learn that India will become what they make of her. Where they decide that the world, too, is their responsibility. Where they discover that the object of knowledge is service. Where they make the resolve that their lives will be used to bind the wounds and repair the spirits of our people, not vaguely people at large, but of individuals one by one."

RAJMOHAN GANDHI

To the teachers

THE WAY AHEAD has been created in response to a request from secondary schools in India for help in the teaching of moral values and in character training.
The aims of this course are:

1. To give the students knowledge of and practical concern for the needs of their own and other nations.
2. To encourage initiative and responsibility.
3. To develop qualities of unselfish leadership.
4. To make normal the discipline and adventure of listening to the Inner Voice and obeying its dictates.
5. To produce the men and women of integrity who will be prepared to undertake to change what is wrong in society, starting with themselves.

Most young people respond when faced with a big enough challenge — a purpose in life which takes all their energy, talents and creative thought. There are many needs in the world today which can only be met by people who are ready to sacrifice and serve unselfishly. We should expect our students to aim for the highest. Most adolescents are idealists at heart and therefore nothing less than the best can provide for their deepest longings and hopes.

This material, we hope, will help you to make your lessons relevant, interesting and challenging. Each topic is a project to help the students think through the ideas put forward and be guided to come to logical conclusions. These should always be the ones which help the students to be stronger, more effective and satisfied people. In this way, too, we have experienced that students begin to find the determination and desire within themselves and with God's help, to live the truths they know to be right. However, we know from our own experience, that the effectiveness of these lessons depends on our quality of life. It is the teacher's simple honesty and sincerity which will affect the students most.

The stakes are great. We are faced with the possible collapse of civilisation around the world. Our task is to arrest and reverse this moral slide. "The truth is that civilisation collapses when the essential reverence for absolute values which religion gives, disappears. ... Men live on the accumulated faith of the past as well as on its accumulated self-discipline. Overthrow these and nothing seems missing at first. ... But something has gone ... the motor which held the society together, the integrity of the human soul, then the rats come out of their holes and begin burrowing under foundations and there is nothing to withstand them." (Dr Monk Gibbon)

All the material included has been used in the classroom by teachers and many of the topics have been suggested by students and teachers. We have also had the valuable experience of using it with students of a teacher training college.

In the next chapter are stories of the experiences teachers have had in the classroom through applying the ideas contained in this course. We include them as many teachers, with whom we have shared them, have found them a great help and encouragement.

The following are a few of the comments from the assessments made by school and college students who took part in the pilot scheme:

School students aged 13 to 16 years
"I have found this term's moral science lessons interesting because we were dealing with things that were really happening in the world."

"Before, I used never to say my prayers. I did not believe in God. Now I say my prayers regularly and I have a *little* belief that there is some great being that is above."

"I have learnt to see through people who are hypocrites and to become less of a hypocrite myself."

"I have learnt to become more tolerant and also to accept others' views."

"I feel I have learnt my place in society through these

lessons and my role as a citizen of the world. I have learnt to feel a concern for my neighbour and a genuine concern for his needs."

College students
The questions posed were: Have these sessions helped you in any way? If so, how?

"Yes! Thank you very much. 1. It has opened my mind to many things I was ashamed to face. 2. It has taught me to be more honest. 3. It has made me change my opinion of others by looking at my own faults. 4. It has put a goal before me in teaching Moral Science which I thought was difficult to teach and had the intention to refuse to teach. But now I will take on the task of imparting some of the changes (that have) over-come me."

"I learnt the importance of giving morals to our children as a teacher and how to admit mistakes and work for the benefit of other people."

"They have made me more aware of myself as a person and how selfish and self-centred man can be. They have given me food for serious thought as to how I am going to lead my life and to review the kind of life I am leading."

It is our conviction that one of the most important aspects of this course is the experience that teachers and students can gain from listening to the deepest thing in their hearts so that God can speak to them on the issues which arise in each topic. This can be experienced through the prayerful silences which should become a natural part of the lessons.

It has also been suggested that a weekly time of corporate prayer should be made available for the students where they can meditate, worship and, if they so wish, share in prayer with others. It was Gandhiji's prayer meetings from which he drew his strength. If our students can experience this in school, it will be a source from which they can continue to draw their strength and direction when they go out into the world of work and added responsibility.

ANN RIGNALL AND JOY WEEKS

Methods

THE COURSE has been divided into two sections. Topics I to X are the basic course which should be studied in the order given. In some topics there are alternative methods of approach, in which case they are so labelled. Some alternatives will be found to be more advanced than others. Topics XI onwards can be taken in any order, according to the needs and the interest of the class. Some may also be used in conjunction with the basic course.

The lecture method should be used as little as possible, and only to stimulate discussion. There should be plenty of participation by the students through discussions and the contribution of ideas. They should be encouraged to think for themselves and to put into practice the ideas they get from the lessons. The teacher should help the students to reach logical conclusions, whilst giving them the freedom to express their ideas. It is important that these are taken seriously and that differing points of view are respected. It has been found that some of the most successful class discussions have been those when students' questions have been answered by each other rather than by the teacher.

QUIZZES AND QUESTIONNAIRES

These are meant to encourage thoughtful and honest answers, rather than what might be considered the 'right' answers. If the teacher wants the students to search deeply into their hearts, then their privacy and confidence must be respected at all costs. There must be an understanding that what is said in these lessons is treated as confidential. This is the only way to build the necessary trust.

GROUP DISCUSSIONS

These help to give everyone the opportunity to express their opinions. The class can be divided into small groups, of preferably no more than ten people, with an appointed leader who has written down the topics or questions to be considered. There should also be a reporter in each group who will keep a record of what is discussed, so that the conclusions of the group can be reported to the whole class later.

PLAY WRITING

If a theme for a play has been suggested, it is often possible to divide the class into small groups. Let them plan an improvisation for ten minutes. Then perform, without scripts, the ideas they have. This can lead to a play being scripted by one or two members of the group, including the suggestions given by those in the audience.

PLAY READINGS

Play readings can be very effective if the cast sits in front of the class and each character stands when on stage and sits when off. No actions need be done but a narrator should be appointed to read the main stage directions.

FILM SHOWS

Some suggestions of possible films are given after the Bibliography. For these to be fully effective, questionnaires should be given to the class to answer and discuss after they have seen the film. It is sometimes helpful before the film to give certain points for the students to look for, without in any way divulging the story. It is therefore essential for the teacher to view the film before using it with a class.

OTHER METHODS

1. Essay writing
2. Collection of pictures and material from newspapers and magazines to make a display of certain topics.
3. Art work
4. Writing of poetry
5. Displays in the classroom or school corridor.

It is advised that every student and teacher has a small notebook in which to write down any ideas he has on personal matters, which he may or may not wish to tell others in public.

Response

Below are the stories of teachers who have tried to put into practice the ideas expressed in this course.

AN EXPERIENCED member of staff in a Bombay secondary school set about making character-building his priority through each lesson he taught. His first experiment was with "honesty".

He knew that a great deal of cheating was taking place during tests and exams. He had given endless lectures on this subject in the past, with no effect. Now he tackled it in a new way. Each time the opportunity presented itself — perhaps a "borrowed" pen or a lie about why homework was not done—he gradually began to help the students to see their actions in the light of needed changes in the school and in the nation. He did not lecture, but asked the class questions concerning these things, encouraging them to say what they thought. The conclusion was reached that a person who was dishonest himself did not have the right to complain about the dishonesty of others.

One day this teacher put a Sanskrit test on the board before the class arrived. When they had all entered, he told them that during the test they could refer to their notes and text books or copy from their neighbours. He said he was going out of the classroom, locking the door and would return at the end of the period.

There was a shocked silence as the teacher walked to the door. Then a boy put up his hand and said, "No, sir."

"Why not?" asked the teacher. "You want to pass your test, don't you?"

"Yes," was the reply.

"Your parents want you to attain high marks. My reputation is at stake, and, what's more, I have given you permission to cheat. So, what's wrong?"

This started a great discussion. Why was it wrong to cheat if the teacher said they could? Their conclusion, after much to and fro, was that cheating was wrong, whatever the circumstances.

The teacher then said, "What are you going to decide to do in the future? You have always known that cheating was wrong but you have done it. Now will you make a decision to do what is right?"

The class all said that they would never cheat again in their Sanskrit tests or exams. Their teacher, however, was not satisfied with this and eventually they gave their word that they would not cheat in *any* tests or exams.

The next day they did their Sanskrit test. However, one of the slower girls was seen by the teacher copying from the most intelligent girl in the class. He said nothing, but, on receiving their marked papers a few days later, the girls discovered that they had both been given zero percent. Another discussion ensued. Was it as wrong to let someone copy from you as it was to copy from someone else? The two girls admitted that they were equally to blame and accepted the punishment of receiving zero.

During the school exams that year the cheating incidents went down in that class by at least 90%. The teacher said that in twenty five years of teaching he had never obtained such a result before.

The following is the story of a teacher, Miss Joyce Kneale, and her work with a difficult class in a state primary school in a very over-crowded area of London. She says of the class that it was "one of the most disobedient, rude and rebellious I have ever known. Frankly I felt helpless with this unpromising material." However, she had learned that God could tell her what to do and that if she obeyed He would act. "I scarcely believed that anything would happen in this situation, but three ideas came. First to give the children an aim outside themselves; second, to see all their families; and third, to set out to change the ringleaders and their families." This is how she achieved her first aim.

"We took as our aim to make the Commonwealth an example of how nations of all colours and creeds could work together. This meant that we had to try to make our part of London a pattern — a tall order if you knew the area.

"One of the first suggestions made was to get rid of all fights. The children got a bit of a shock when I asked them all to write down the name of someone they didn't like very much. Very few had trouble in finding a name. Next I asked them to write down why they didn't like the person. They all had perfectly marvellous reasons. The final question was more difficult. 'What are you going to do about it?' Many ideas came — very different for each person, but all had at least one step that could be taken towards the building of a friendship to replace the animosity."

Earlier the children had learnt that "sorry" was a useful word for ending fights. Miss Kneale noticed that the fights and viciousness began to get less. She also says, "It was interesting to see those who earlier had played alone, being absorbed into corporate games. Gangs with an exclusiveness about them began to disappear. There grew a keen desire to break them up, even when they were from other classes."

Learning about the different countries of the Commonwealth followed, and they started with India. "Of course they knew about the starving children there. I told them that one way to help was if people became honest and trustworthy. This, I explained, was not easy. In fact I had found myself to be dishonest. Once was over stealing from my father's shop — chocolates, dried fruit and other tempting delicacies. Another was going into the cinema for half-price when long past the adult age for entry.

" 'How many of you have ever taken things that were not yours?' I asked. Seventy-five percent put up their hands. 'Would you list them?' I suggested. So they did. Almost the entire class made lists of items they had stolen from parents, friends and shops. At this point I took the chance of telling them how I had repaid money for all that I had taken and had apologised personally. I gave them a quiz which ended, 'What can you do about the things you have stolen? When will you do it?'

"Every person except one made amends. The brightest boy in the class decided to go back to a large store with money to pay for some items he had stolen. He was afraid, so I went to give him support. The manager was surprised that he had come and thanked him.

"He told me privately afterwards that thousands of pounds are being lost every year through pilfering. ... Another little girl influenced her friend at another school to return money to a shop. The one boy who had not followed the path of restitution was later in serious trouble with the police but all the rest became utterly trustworthy.

"Then George, who was usually a difficult boy to handle, had a good idea about India. He thought people in the Commonwealth should stop being greedy. He brought a box from home to collect money, not from the extra that could be coaxed out of the parents, but from the money the children had intended to spend on sweets. The money was sent to people in India, known to me, who ensured it went to those in need. This child had been going to a psychologist. From that day he has not been back to him. The effect of these actions on the general behaviour has been striking. Fidgeting disappeared and there was a new ability to concentrate in the class.

"We followed this theme in every lesson and the class was fascinated. All the experiences they had had during the term were included in a play we wrote for Christmas. It told the story of a ship on its way to a Commonwealth Conference. Five of the children took the parts of stowaways. Their adventures brought them into contact with children from many Commonwealth countries. One child, who had been a moaner and groaner, decided after seeing the Nativity scene, to quit the moans and think about her friends. Another, a girl who never helped at home, offered her hands to do the housework and the cooking. The Mayor was there. At the end of the play he got up and asked to speak. He was very moved. It had reminded him, he said, of many things he had forgotten.

"It seemed a natural next step that we should go to the Houses of Parliament and hear more of what it means to be a responsible citizen. So we asked our Member of Parliament to take the class round. After this visit, the Member of Parliament asked the children to write a book about Parliament. In it there was to be a chapter on how to be a good citizen. When I took the six best along to the Houses of Parliament to show him, it was this chapter that intrigued him. They simply told him about their own experiences — the need to pay debts, to be honest, keep their bedroom and the district tidy and cure viciousness. The quality of the books was such that he decided to take them to the Speaker, who was so thrilled that he sent a special letter to the school in which he said that they were among the highest standard of work in London. He also sent a book written by himself on democracy for each of the six children.

"The class was now in a position to give what they had learned to many people. One man who came to meet them was a leader of Cyprus at the time when it received its independence. He had since been very disillusioned by what had happened there. The children told him all they had been doing and it meant a great deal, he said."

A class which had been a problem now had found their part in building up the neighbourhood. Personality problems began to be solved and academic standards went up. Every lesson had been used to achieve this.

The following is a conviction of a teacher of many years teaching experience.

"I taught for five years in an expensive school for the daughters of professional or wealthy business men. These facts clearly emerged:

"Many of the children did not believe that their parents loved them, even though they gave them expensive presents.

"Many of the girls resented being 'shown-off' at parties. Some of them were sure, even at fourteen years of age, that money did not satisfy and despised their parents' pre-occupation with it. They resented above all the fact that they had been spoiled. They felt untrained for living, disliked and insecure. They felt that parents try to buy their children's love. The children knew this was false.

"I was astonished to find out how much they knew about the dishonesty in the lives of their parents. Most of the girls in a certain class cheated in an examination when I first went to the school. They said, 'Father cheats in his income tax so why shouldn't we cheat in exams?' When we talked about the cost to the country of that kind of dishonesty most of the class came to me and said they had decided never to cheat again.

"One other fact I came across was this. Even by fourteen

years of age some of these children felt there was nothing to look forward to. 'We've had everything,' they said. 'There's nothing left to try.'

"I concluded from remarks like this, which came pouring out of the children, that it was their parents who most of all needed to do some 'stock-taking'. But since it was often not possible to talk to the parents how did one tackle the situation in the children? Sometimes I have known that the parents were completely to blame for the bitterness and frustration in the children. What does one do in these circumstances?

"I have taken the line that always, no matter what the provocation, hate is wrong. Surprisingly I have found that young people accept this. Also we have realised together that it is up to us to build for the next generation the kind of world we would like to see. A fifteen-year-old girl wrote in an essay, 'We teenagers, if we will live by high moral standards, will affect the standards of youth for generations to come.'"

To the students

This is a possible introduction to the whole course which teachers can use for their classes. It can be read to them as it is or the ideas it contains can be put into the teacher's own words.

THERE IS much to be done in the world. We need to provide enough food, enough houses and enough work, so that everybody in the world has the necessities of life. Such a task is possible. Yet it is often hate, selfishness, greed, bitterness and lust in people that causes the shortage of these necessities. We need to help those who are hungry in spirit — to give hope and purpose to those who lack them, to heal the hurts and bind up the broken hearts. Anyone and everyone can have a part in doing this.

Through this course we have tried to help you find how to undertake this task effectively. We have tried to answer some of the questions we have been asked, such as:

"How can we understand more about what is happening in the world?"

"What can I, just one person, do when the problems we face are so great?"

"I know what is right and what is wrong, but can you help me to want to do what is right?"

"Why should we be honest in school when everyone else is corrupt?"

"Honesty doesn't pay."

"How do you know that God exists?"

"How can we learn to have the courage to stand up for what we believe in?"

We hope that this course will help you to think about life — how we live it and for what it is meant — and come to decisions which will help you when you leave school and join the world of work and increased responsibility.

The world is much in need of men and women of integrity who will take responsibility and give selfless leadership in whatever walk of life they choose. We believe that all of you can become these men and women.

The world in which we live

AIMS

To take a careful and objective look at what is wrong in the world and to pick out how much of it is due to the simple problems of human nature. It is then easier to see each individual's responsibility and the part he/she can play in putting right what is wrong, starting with themselves in their homes, schools, colleges and communities.

DEVELOPMENT

Man's achievements in the last hundred years have been amazing. Ask the class to write down the major new inventions they can think of in the last fifty years.

It is a fact that 90% of the scientists who have ever lived are living in our lifetime (although the other 10% does include most of the greatest names in scientific thought).

There is also a great increase in the speed of development of technology. From the discovery of electricity in the last century to its industrial application it took fifty years. For radio to be made industrially available it took a little over twenty years. For atomic energy there was five or six years between discovery and practical application. For the Laser ray it has taken three years.

What are the ways in which science and technology are helping to end poverty and hunger in the world?

Yet in spite of this there are still many problems in the world. Hunger and poverty still exist. In some ways science and technology are contributing to these problems.

How is this so?

At this point there might be the chance to discuss a little the question of pollution.

If man uses science and technology selfishly — for his own personal or national benefit only — then other people will suffer. We have reached such a level of development that nations *must* consider each other and work together.

"It is even possible that recognition of our environmental interdependence ... could, positively, give us that sense of community, of belonging, and living together, without which no human society can be built up, survive and prosper. ... It is only in our own day that astronomers, physicists, geologists, chemists, biologists, anthropologists, ethnologists and archeologists have all combined in a single witness of advanced science to tell us that ... we do indeed belong to a single system ... depending for its survival on the balance and health of the total system." Barbara Ward, *Only One Earth*.

What are the problems in the world today which need to be answered?

Which ones of them apply to this country?

(A study of the newspapers would help to provide material for this[1]).

Take one particular problem named by the class, preferably one which applies to this country and help the class to work out the main reasons underlying this problem. It is important not to stop at the political and economic reasons, but to see that it is the wrong things in human nature which cause these problems.

Find out what part greed, selfishness, hate, fear, dishonesty, immorality, laziness etc. play in the problem you discuss.

"If everybody was well housed, well clothed and well fed the problems of our world would be solved."

Discuss this statement with the class.

Consider whether the privileged classes of this country — those who have all they want materially — are the most satisfied and most honest people in the country.

Get the class to consider the picture they have of the affluent nations of the world — are these nations free from

---

[1] Also see under Activities, opposite.

industrial unrest, suicide, divorce, race conflicts, divided families etc.?

From such consideration will come the fact that material prosperity does not of itself bring satisfaction and peace.

Stress the fact that it is human nature which we need to tackle if we are really to bring a cure to what is wrong in the world.

Having dealt with these big problems it is important to bring the whole subject down-to-earth. The problems of the world can often be found immediately around us in our homes, our school and class. Ask the class to write the answers to the following questions:

1. Name three problems in your home, school or local community which you would like to see answered.
2. How do you think these problems could be solved?
3. What do you think you could do, either individually or as a class, to help in bringing a solution?

Get any who are willing to read out what they have written. Discuss with the class any practical steps which could be taken. Encourage them to follow up their thoughts (if they are helpful ones!) and see if they can bring some answers to the problems. Life is much more interesting if you can solve problems rather than just discuss them.

ACTIVITIES

Prepare a class display of cuttings and pictures to illustrate the theme "The World as It Is". Have a map of the world and mark on it the places concerned with the cuttings and pictures. It helps the students if they are continually aware of what is happening in the world. This could be done by a permanent display of this kind, which is brought up-to-date every week. Maybe certain sections of the class could take it in turn to be responsible.

DISCUSSION SUBJECT

Divide the class into small discussion groups to consider this quotation:

"A race which has grown up intellectually must grow up morally or perish" Dr B. H. Streeter.

Use the following questions as a basis for discussion:

1. Is it true that we have remained static as far as moral development is concerned e.g. are we less selfish, less greedy, less prejudiced than our forbears?
2. Technological advancement is obvious, but are we equipped with more wisdom, better judgement, higher moral values than those before us?
3. Have there been instances in history of decadent nations perishing? If so, where and when? Do you think our civilisation is in danger of perishing? Give the reasons for your answer.

At the end get each discussion group to report back their findings to the whole class.

RESOURCE MATERIAL

Some major discoveries of the last fifty years:

1926 Television first demonstrated
First liquid fuel rocket produced
1927 Colour television demonstrated
Vitamin B isolated
1928 First Mickey Mouse cartoon film
Penicillin discovered
First talking films shown in cinema
Latex foam developed
1929 Description of electric charges in the brain — beginning of electro-encephalogy
1930 Yellow fever serum effectively used
Experiments commenced for jet engines
1931 Electric razor invented
1932 Vitamin C isolated
1933 Influenza virus isolated
Discovery of polythene
1934 Poliomyelitis vaccine discovered
1935 Radar invented
1937 First successful jet engine tested
1938 Beginnings of radio astronomy
Nylon discovered
First practical ball point pen made

1939   First jet aircraft flown
1941   Terylene first produced
1942   First nuclear reactor constructed
1945   First atomic bomb exploded
1946   Invention of electric blanket
1947   Oral treatment of leprosy found
1948   Supersonic speeds in aircraft first reached
1951   First peaceful uses of atomic energy
1952   First hydrogen bomb exploded
       First commercial jet airline service
1954   Solar battery developed
1957   First artificial Earth satellite launched and first inter-
       continental ballistic missile
1959   Hovercraft invented
1961   First men in space
1963   Vaccine for measles developed
1965   First commercial communication satellite launched
       First space walk
1967   First heart transplant
       First laser surgery operating theatre built
1969   First man landed on the moon

Ways in which science is helping to end poverty and hunger
in the world:

Irrigation   New strains of crops and seeds
Artificial Fertilisers   Education of villagers through
Flood Control   television and satellites
Control of soil erosion

POLLUTION

This is a major problem in the developed and industrialised
countries, but some study of it can help the developing
countries not to run into the same problem.

AIR POLLUTION

The main source of this is the generation of electricity and
the motor car. In the US pollutants in the air amount each
year to about a ton for every American. Such pollution not
only affects the health of the people but can affect the climate
also. It can cut out sunshine and increase rain, which in turn
affects agriculture. At the same time the heat being generated

from industrial activity and rising into the air could raise the
temperature of the earth several degrees.

WATER POLLUTION

This can happen in lakes, rivers and the sea through the
depositing of waste material from industry. If too much
sewage for instance goes into a river, the bacteria in the river
have to use up more oxygen in order to decompose this sewage.
Thus the river loses its capacity for supporting living things
such as fish. This is true, for example, of all the rivers around
the paper-making city of Fuiji in Japan. Water is also used
for cooling in certain industries. This hot water is then poured
back into the rivers and raises the level of the temperature.
This too can impose sharp changes on the aquatic life in the
river. There is the danger of chemicals such as pesticides
leaking into the rivers. Between 1960 and 1963 it is estimated
that ten to fifteen million fish were killed in the Mississippi
river because of this.

In modern life there is the problem of what to do with
waste materials, of which there are many. For instance in the
US each year there are 48 billion metal cans, 26 billion bottles,
65 billion metal bottle caps and 7 million junked cars to
dispose of! Man in his demand for the material things of life
and in his belief that he can control his environment has
created many difficulties in the world. One example is that the
demand for paper and for more cultivable land has meant that
large areas of forest in the world have been cleared. This has
resulted in flooding and in soil erosion.

It is calculated that over the whole world one inch of good
top soil is lost through erosion every three years. In the Ivory
Coast in West Africa, a cleared piece of land was compared
with a forest piece of land next to it. In one year, the cleared
land lost through erosion 93 tons of soil per hectare. In the
adjacent forested land, 24 tons of soil were lost per hectare.

We have to be careful that we do not upset the balance of
nature. One example in Malaya concerns spraying to kill the
malaria mosquito. This nearly caused an outbreak of plague
and caused roofs to fall in. This was because the spraying killed
and reduced the number of roaches, which reduced the number
of geckos, which reduced the number of cats, as they fed on

the geckos. As there were fewer cats, the numbers of rats increased and with them the plague-bearing lice. If rat poison had been put down, the lice would have left the rats and gone on to people thus causing an outbreak of plague. However, instead the authorities brought in more cats. As far as the roofs were concerned, the leaf-eating caterpillar increased, because the wasps who preyed on them were decimated by the spraying. Therefore the caterpillars kept on eating at the supports of the roofs.

Scientists have discovered ways in which to change the climates of areas. However, if you change the climate of one area for the better, it can change the climate of another area for the worse, e.g. scientists have worked out that a dam could be built across the Bering Straits. Then the cold Arctic water could be pumped out and the warm Atlantic water could be pumped in. This would mean that huge areas of Northern Canada and Russia, which are now permanently frozen, would be capable of growing grass, and huge herds of cattle could be kept. The basins of the Rivers Don and Volga in Russia would become sub-tropical, Britain would become warmer and damper and the US may become too warm for comfort. Grass might even grow in the Sahara. However, the North Pacific would become much colder and what would happen to the rice fields of Japan or the rubber plantations of Malaysia?

Further information on this subject:
Only One Earth by Barbara Ward and Rene Dubos
The Doomsday Book by G. R. Taylor

Who is to blame?

AIMS As for Ia

DEVELOPMENT

There should be a large map of the world in front of the class
for this topic.

> Where is there trouble in the world these days?
> Where are there conflicts?
> What are they about?
> Do you know how they started? Who is to blame?
> What is being done to try and solve them?
>> Use newspapers to find out more details or additional
>> information about countries not yet mentioned.
> What are the things that you and your friends argue
> about?
> How do your quarrels start?
> What starts quarrels at home?

Read this poem to the class or have four students prepare it
beforehand so that it can be read in parts.

HOW DO WARS BEGIN?

A little girl was playing by the fireside one winter's night,
Playing as all children will to her heart's delight.
Her mummy and her daddy were sitting by the firelight
When she asked them both this question as any child might.
"Mummy, daddy tell me please, now I'm almost ten,
Why do nations go to war time and time again?

Why must Johnny be a soldier boy? How do all our wars begin?
Why do nations get themselves into the mess they're in?"
Daddy puffed his pipe awhile and let the fire grow cold.
"The reason is quite simple dear, they want each other's gold,
Each other's wealth, each other's land, everyone wants more,
Over economic questions dear, nations go to war."
Said the mummy of the little girl knitting by the fire,
"The reason is quite different dear, now that you enquire,
People come from many different lands, many different creeds
    and skins,
Over questions of religion dear, every war begins."

Daddy tapped his pipe and said, "No, that isn't true,
All your reasons simply are a woman's point of view."
Mummy smiled, "Religion is the cause of every war."
Daddy snapped, "It's economics, like I said before."
"No it isn't," Mummy said. "Yes it is," said Dad.
"No it isn't." "Yes it is." "No it isn't." "Yes it is."
"No it isn't." "Yes it is."
"STOP . . . Now I know," said the little girl, with a great big
    grin,
"You have shown me clearly how all our wars begin."
But little girls and little boys, the world is not so bad
'Cos you needn't copy everything from your mum and dad,
We can build a world of peace for all, better than we knew
    before,
Starting by our fireside to answer every war.

Quarrels can end with everyone being friends again, or they
can end leaving those who quarrelled as enemies. What makes
the difference?

Can you give an example of a quarrel that ended either
way from your experience?

Have you had any arguments or quarrels that have left
you feeling angry or bitter towards someone else? Is there
anything you can do about it? When will you do it?

Who is to blame when a quarrel starts?

People often say, "It takes two to make a fight". When
it involves others we agree with this. Do we agree when it is
we who are involved? Whom do we tend to blame?

When I point my finger at my neighbour, there are three more pointing back at me.

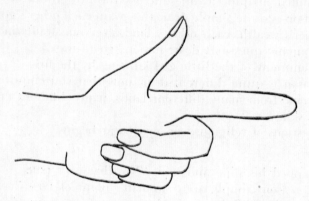

Maybe I am three times as bad.

A wise old man once was asked, "Who do you think is to blame for the mess the world is in?" He went away and thought for a while. Then he called the people together. He held up a picture with its back to the audience saying that here was the portrait of the person who was to blame for all that was going wrong. He invited his audience to come up one by one and see for themselves who it was. They did so. Some returned to their seats very thoughtful and others were indignant and angry. Of whom was the portrait?

(The teacher should have a large mirror which looks like a picture from the back. Each student can come up and discover for himself.)

Countries which are at peace also have troubles. What are they? (Famine, industrial disputes, lack of freedom of speech, poverty, permissiveness and student unrest etc.)

ACTIVITIES

Write and act some plays illustrating, "How Do Wars Begin?"

Is there any way in which the class can meet and hear from people from the countries they have talked about most, or see films? This would help them to understand the human issues at stake and widen their knowledge of the world. This is an important aspect of the course as we are all more interested in changing ourselves if we see a big enough reason.

What makes life worth living?

AIMS

To find out what are the most important values in life and how to apply them in our own lives.

DEVELOPMENT

(In the lesson before beginning this subject, ask the class to bring at least one advertisement each from a magazine etc. choosing ones which give some indication of what the advertisers feel is important in life e.g. Product A makes you lovelier each day. Buy Product B for a happier home etc.)

Ask the class to write down either the names of six people they admire or the type of people they admire. If they write down names, get them also to write why they admire these people.

Write up on the board the qualities named by the class and then let them copy this list, as they will need to refer back to it later.

Now turn to a study of the advertisements. From them make up two lists on the board:

1. The qualities of life which the advertisements say are important.
2. The sort of people the advertisements encourage us to be.

Compare list 1. with the important qualities of life listed earlier. Find out how many qualities are on both lists. It will probably be very few. Get the class to suggest reasons for this fact. This will probably lead to some discussion of the aims of advertising. What are they? Are advertisers more concerned about a) selling their product, or b) the type of society they are creating?

Study list 2. Does the class consider this is the type of person they want to be? Let them give their reasons. Consider also whether this is the type of person the world needs to solve its problems.

By now it should be clear that the materialistic society exerts great pressure on all of us.

Emphasise this fact with the class. All the time we are being urged to possess things we haven't got and perhaps cannot afford and to be the sort of people we are not.

Once people have some material possessions they want more. It seems to be true that the more they have the more they want. Ask the class to consider whether their richer friends are their happier friends. If so, is it because they have more money? If not, why do you think this is so?

One leader of an African country asked, "How can we have prosperity without decadence?" He meant how could he build a country where everyone had enough clothes, good homes and enough food without becoming selfish and greedy. Ask the class how they would answer this question.

It is said, "If you don't stand for something, you will fall for anything." Ask each member of the class to write down the values that they are going to stand for. This should not be a list of good ideas, but the values which they are going to apply in their own lives. The world is too full of people who say they believe in one thing, but live in a completely opposite way.

No one can *make* us live the way we should. It is up to each one of us to *decide*. We need a big enough reason if we are going to stick to it. Let the class write down the reasons which would make them give up their selfish way of living. Some of them may be willing to read out these reasons to the rest of the class.

THINGS TO DO

Make posters of pictures, drawings, cuttings etc. showing:
1. The materialistic world of advertising
2. The values which the class feel are important in the world, and to each of our lives.

A vision for India

AIMS

To find out what sort of nation we want ours to be, so that we know what we are aiming to achieve through our lives.

DEVELOPMENT

Ask the class to write down a description of the country they would like India to be.

Study the following passage written by a group of young Indians:

"Despite her blemishes we love India. But we want to work to remove those blemishes.

"We want to see an India where every family has a decent house and every house the spirit of a real home. An India of attractive (and clean and sanitary) villages and towns, with nutritious food and drinking water for all.

"A land that has roads without holes, administration without corruption, business without greed, industry without stoppages, products without adulteration, hospitals without congestion and examinations without cheating.

"A land where men treat one another, without exception, as royal souls, instead of some being treated as gods and others as dogs. Where wealth-worship gives way to the service of men, and indolence to intelligent labour.

"Where belief in the timelessness of certain values is not perverted into a disregard for punctuality; where courtesy replaces harshness in conversation.

"And where compassion melts the hardness of heart that has allowed us for so long to live alongside human degradation.

"India does not live for Indians alone.

"The world seems to need India.

"Her destiny is to build bridges between Asia and the West, between the Communist and the non-Communist worlds and within the vast Asian continent, between the largely Muslim regions to our west and the Buddhist-influenced lands to the east.

"Geography and history and the culture, complexion and aspirations of her population seem to call for an India which does this."[1]

If possible let every member of the class have a copy of *Handbook of Hope*, so that they can really study it. In order to pinpoint certain issues, ask the class the following questions. Most of them open up large topics and the teacher can decide how far to go into them, according to the age and the interest of the class. Many of the points will be developed in further lessons.

QUESTIONNAIRE

1. What are the blemishes in India which need to be removed?
2. What do you think should be the spirit of a real home? How can this spirit be created?
3. What does it mean "To treat each other, without exception, as royal souls."?
   How do we treat people whom we respect? Is respect given to people solely through their position in society or are there other reasons as well? Is respect automatically given to certain people or does it have to be earned?
   What difference would this attitude of "treating everyone like royal souls" have on the country?
   What things would have to change in your life if you were to adopt this attitude towards people?
4. Write down the values which you think are timeless. Why?
5. Punctuality has been called "The courtesy of kings". What does this mean?
6. Why do you think India, geographically, historically and

---

[1] *Handbook of Hope* edited by Padmini Kirtane (see Bibliography).

culturally is suited to bridge the gap "between the Communist and the non-Communist worlds and within the
vast Asian continent, between the largely Muslim regions
to our west and the Buddhist influenced lands to the east"?
(See the material under Resource Material as giving some
ideas for this. However, let the students give their own ideas
first.)
7. What do you think your country could give to the rest of
the world — not necessarily material goods?

ACTIVITIES

Make a classroom display of the ways in which people are
trying to improve things in the country.

RESOURCE MATERIAL

INDIA AND ASIA
by Rajmohan Gandhi *Himmat,* 21 June, 1974

India's influence in Asia is not as large as it could be. A recent
visit to South East Asia convinced me that it can be increased,
and also that it can be used for great aims.

What are the channels that connect India with Asia? For
a start there are the Indian communities in virtually every
country. Sri Lanka has a huge minority of Indian origin.
Malaysia has a sizeable percentage. Singapore's Tamils, Malaya-
lees and Sikhs are fewer but significant enough. Thailand has
Sikh watchmen and "bhaiya" milk vendors. Vietnam, Cambodia
and Laos have Tamil-speaking Hindus and Muslims, and
Sindhi businessmen. The latter abound also in Hong Kong
and the Philippines.

Far to the South, in the Pacific, Indians are actually a
majority in Fiji, and form an interesting vegetable-farming
element in New Zealand.

To our West, in the Gulf countries and in Iran and the
Arab world, Indian accountants, clerks, maids, doctors,
engineers and businessmen earn handsomely....

Asian Indians could become a cementing force rather
than a thorn in the flesh, an asset rather than a liability. The
prospect would depend on what they are committed to. Which
do they love more, money or the country they work in? What
portion of their earnings do they give, in taxes or voluntarily

in charity, to their adopted countries? What portion do they send to relatives in India illegally? Are they daringly honest or are they after quick money made on the side? Are they free from rivalries and dissensions, and thus able to assist towards the unity and strength of their new country?

Burma's lesson can easily be forgotten. South Indians and Bengalis and people from most parts of India had settled in that country, which for some time was linked with India.

Not all the Indians in Burma were greedy, and only a tiny minority were rich. Yet they failed to win the trust and affection of Burma. They were judged self-seeking and arrogant and virtually every single one of them was sent out.

Governments commit excesses. ... But we would also do well to recognise that Indians have often alienated the general public before governments have acted against them.

The physical presence of Indians is not, of course, the only connection between Asia and India. Buddhism, born in India, has moulded for centuries the lives of giant and vital Asian lands. Bodhigaya and Sarnath mean far more to Japanese and Thais, Laotians and the people of Sri Lanka than we realise. And despite all that the people of East and South East Asia may feel about the poverty, frustrations and inefficiency of India, they do not forget that it was India that nourished the Buddha. Respect for India's qualities of the spirit survives; nations continue to expect, even if they think they do not always receive, a moral and ethical stance from India.

We have barely understood the vast potential of the link with East Asia this fantastic figure who lived 2500 years ago has given us. ... Asian idealism, alive and kicking despite the beatings it has taken, still views India as a land where moral standards might prevail. A shift, however slight to begin with, in business, administrative or political practices inside India would act like a magnet to which Asia's Buddhist lands would willingly allow themselves to be drawn.

The blinding speed of Japanese economic progress, now arrested by the oil crisis, was never able to satisfy Japan's heart. Some Japanese continue to look wistfully, even if not too confidently, towards India for answers.

Nor need we rule out the interest of China in the philosophy and practice of a country that once did send Buddhism to the Middle Kingdom (China).

A Vietnamese public figure, yearning for the right way for his country, spoke of what he felt was the mighty contribution that India and China could together make to mankind. India, he thought, had vision and wisdom, even if Indians talked more and did less than they should.

The Chinese had practical skills, industriousness and the aesthetic sense. Perhaps the nations of Indochina would assist in creating an India-China partnership.

If Buddhism is a bond with nations east of us, Islam allies us to West Asia (and to Bangla Desh, Indonesia and Malaysia).

Islam was imported into India, but for centuries it has been a profound and pervasive indigenous force. India's non-Muslims are as proud as her Muslims of the legacy of culture and brotherhood, of nobility, art and architecture that Islam has given her. In Islamic lands the Indian, whether a Muslim or not, can easily feel at home.

What is to be India's contribution to the thinking now in progress in oil-rich Islamic lands on what is widely called the problem of having too much money? Is there not something in the words and spirit of Islam that can be a steer and a guide? The West has not given a convincing display of what to do with affluence. Can Iran and the Arab lands do better? Can India have a prudent part in evolving a new thinking?

As I am so is my nation

AIM

To bring the class to a decision to become the sort of people the world needs and to take the practical steps necessary to make this a reality.

DEVELOPMENT

Ask the class:

What do you do when you feel that things are wrong:

Grumble about them?
Blame someone else?
Join in a protest or demonstration?
See what you can do to put things right?
Shrug your shoulders and do nothing?

Which of these are likely to change the situation?
What are the ways in which people protest about what is wrong?
Discuss the methods — gheraos, strikes, sit-ins, demonstrations etc.

Use the newspapers to find recent examples of them, not only in this country. How effective are these methods in permanently changing what is wrong?

Look at the effectiveness in the long term as well as the short. Does the whole nation benefit or just a section of it? Some mention should be made of Gandhiji's methods. Why were these effective?

A man who was a student leader during the struggle for independence tells of an interview he had with Gandhiji. He visited him to ask for his blessing on a strike they had organised. "When I explained the purpose of my visit, he said an interesting thing. 'Yes I am interested that you want to go on strike, but number one, be sure that the cause for which you are going on strike is based on nothing but pure and absolute truth.' The second thing he said was, 'Be sure if you go on this strike that you have no hatred of the Englishman, that you have no hate or bitterness towards anyone in your heart.' And the third thing he said was, 'Love the police and those who will be your enemies on the other side.' Then he said, 'If you are absolutely convinced about the truth of your cause, then you can also be sure that God and His strength will be behind you'."

Many people have tried to change the wrongs in society by changing the economic and political system in their country. How far has this been successful? Mention could be made of Solzhenitsyn and the other Russian dissidents. In one of Solzhenitsyn's books, *Cancer Ward*, one character says, "We thought it was enough to change the mode of production and immediately people would change as well. But did they change? The hell they did. They did not change a bit."

It is clear from experience that as yet human nature has not been changed simply by changing the system. For instance if everything was organised in the school as you think it should be, would that turn you into a better person?

The dilemma of our age is:

EVERYONE WANTS TO SEE THE OTHER FELLOW CHANGE
EVERY NATION WANTS TO SEE THE OTHER NATION CHANGE
BUT EVERYONE IS WAITING FOR THE OTHER TO BEGIN

What do you think is the answer to this? Where do you think is the first place which all of us can start to change?

IF YOU WANT TO SEE THINGS DIFFERENT THE PLACE TO START IS WITH YOURSELF

Ask the students to write down the following statement:

INDIA IS MADE UP OF 600 MILLION PEOPLE LIKE ME

Now consider the following:

1. What sort of person do you think you are? Write down your good qualities and your bad ones too. Be really honest.
2. Is it true that your country is like you? In what ways is it?
3. If you want your country to become different, then where can you start yourself? When will you start making these improvements?
4. When you start to do this, you will discover that you have found the answer to the often asked question, "But what can I, just *one* person, do?"

DISCUSSION QUESTION

How can we make our class an example of how we would like the country to be? Make some practical decisions. Think how to spread these ideas through the school.

We don't have to wait until we are perfect before we start tackling the problem around us. We only need to take the first steps that we see. The following story is what some students in Madras were able to do.

STUDENT POWER — NEW STYLE

In Madras in February 1971, there was a dispute in Standard Motors, which had closed the factory for nine months. The company had lost Rs. 70 lakhs and 1,700 families were starving as no wages had been paid for that time. A group of college students decided to take action to resolve this situation. They knew nothing about industry, but they had been experimenting in changing things in their own lives.

Firstly, they went to see the Industries Minister. One of the students apologised to him for words he had used to him on a past occasion. This set the trend for the talks. The Minister said that if the students could help management and labour to find a solution the government would not stand in the way of re-opening the factory.

Next they saw the workers in their homes. At first the workers were antagonistic and asked, "Where were you for the past nine months?" but ultimately the students gained their trust. The legal adviser to the union was persuaded to put forward some new proposals. The Chairman of the company said that he could spare them five minutes, but kept them for an hour. The experience of change told to him by some of the students moved him very much.

Over the following days they visited the people involved in the discussions and managed to prevent a total breakdown of the talks when disagreements arose. As one student said, "We provided the communications necessary for better human relations." Finally a week later *The Times of India* in a front page story announced the re-opening of the factory under the headline, "Student Power — New Style". The *Economic Times* of Bombay reported, "This is perhaps the first time that a major industrial dispute in this country has been solved by student persuasion."

The students themselves said, "All we did was to help the different parties, management, labour and the government, find solutions for themselves. We did this on the basis of what is right rather than who is right."

With an older age group, this story might lead on to a discussion on whether there are any situations which they are meant to tackle together. With a younger age group the following story might be more applicable to them:

This is the story of an event in a school in the southern part of the Sudan, which was a long way from the capital city and the seat of government.

One day the children were told that a certain minister of the government was coming to the school. He was touring the local area and was trying to introduce two matters of policy which were unacceptable to the people and causing distress to them. The question was how should he be welcomed in the school? Could anything be done to change his mind on these matters? The school was in the habit of being silent together and seeking God's help and so they did it on this occasion. After some time of silence a small girl said, "God says we are to make him happy." How? Over the next days a programme emerged.

It became clear that the headmistress should only welcome the minister and then the young staff and the children would take over. He would not talk about matters of policy to them!

The minister and his escort arrived. One hundred girls in green ran out to encircle his car, each waving a golden daisy which they had picked from the flower beds as they ran. They helped him out and clapped and laughed and cheered. The minister looked a little bewildered. The children opened the way for the headmistress to greet him.

With these formalities over, the children closed around him and led him to the school. His escort and the headmistress were left standing. "Would you care for a cool drink?" she asked, as she led the way to the house.

The secretary said, "The minister is only staying fifteen minutes." The headmistress smiled. "Perhaps we should leave him with the children. They have a plan," she said.

The group sat and chatted. At intervals the secretary went to see what was happening. He returned saying, "He seems very happy." Eventually two hours later the minister re-appeared with a small company of children. He was laughing and thanking them. As the headmistress met him, he said, "All I can say is that this is a happy place!" On being offered some refreshment he said, "The children have served me with all I need. Thank you for this happy time. We are very late and we must go."

No mention had been made of his two points of policy which had been causing great anxiety everywhere he had been. Neither did he mention them for the rest of his tour, but seemed to appreciate all that was being done for and by the children. In fact these points of policy were entirely dropped by the government and not heard of again.

Later the headmistress heard the details of the children's programme, which had included serving him with his national food, prepared for him by the senior girls. The children's comment on the outcome was, "It works. He was happy."

ACTIVITIES

1. Write some short plays with the title, "As I am so is my nation".
2. Make illustrated wall posters on the "dilemma of our age", "Everybody wants to see the other person change ..." etc. Each poster could illustrate one line and then be put up in the correct order on the corridor or the classroom wall.

Why absolute standards?

AIMS

To discover the absolute moral standards against which humans must learn to judge their thought and action if they are to be equal to the challenges and opportunities in today's world.

DEVELOPMENT

In life we have to make a whole series of choices. There are the big ones—such as? Let the class give examples (e.g. choice of career, marriage). There are small ones which we have to make every day (e.g. whether we are going to be on time for school or not).

Ask the students to make a list of all the decisions they have had to make since they woke up, e.g. what to eat for breakfast, whether to get up when they were called, etc.

By the choices you make you form your character.

Sow a thought — reap an act.
Sow an act — reap a habit.
Sow a habit — reap a character.
Sow a character — reap a destiny.

Get the class to write this down.

Example:
A boy sees a pen. The *thought* comes to steal it. He does so. The *act* is done. He is not caught and he steals again. It becomes easier each time that he does it. He has to think about it less and less. So stealing becomes a *habit*. He acquires

the *character* of a thief. He may get caught at some time and put into prison and so his *destiny* is set.

On what do we base our choices:

On what most people seem to do?
On what I want to do?
On what my conscience tells me?
On what other people think?

Absolute standards are accepted as normal in many areas of life. Get the class to give examples of some of these areas. Study the following examples:

1. Space travel has developed to an extraordinary degree. Could this have happened if the scientists did not have *absolute* standards with which to calculate and measure?

2. Doctors now use some very strong drugs to cure certain illnesses. Would they be able to use these drugs if they were not able to rely on *absolute* standards in their preparation?

3. If one gives something to be made by a craftsman, a tailor or a carpenter, one is rightly dissatisfied if the garment is not exactly the correct size or if the table has one leg shorter than the other three. These men need to use *absolute* standards of measurement.

4. (a) A parachute that nearly opens is worse than none.
   (b) Food made of bad ingredients may look all right but one cannot eat it.
   (c) A boat that nearly floats ... etc.

There are also standards set in activities such as sports. Why do we have rules on the sports field? What would happen if the rules changed every time we played or if everyone had their own rules? In other areas of life however we have double standards:

Example:

Students often cheat in their tests in order to get better marks and avoid hard work. But if they go to a shop and find they have been cheated they get very annoyed.

Discuss:

Why do we expect higher standards of other people than we do of ourselves? Is this fair? What should we do?

As a space scientist or a tailor judges his work by absolute standards, it is surely logical that we also accept absolute standards against which to judge our behaviour. How do we usually judge our behaviour? Let the students give their answer to this.

Sometimes we compare ourselves with others. For instance we say, "He's much more selfish than I am." Is this good enough? It means we don't really have to change because we are always better than a lot of other people!

However, we could look at *absolute* standards and say "Have I always been absolutely honest? Have I always been absolutely unselfish?" That will show us exactly where we stand and how far we are off course.

We have mentioned honesty and unselfishness as two absolute standards. Which other standards of behaviour are needed? The students should write down their suggestions.

One man looked through Holy scriptures and classified four standards which he believed incorporated the most important aspects of man's behaviour and which could help him to live an effective life. These were:

ABSOLUTE HONESTY   ABSOLUTE UNSELFISHNESS
ABSOLUTE PURITY   ABSOLUTE LOVE

Can the students' ideas be included in these?

Life is a journey. We could say that we are on the ship of life and these four standards are the four points of the compass. We are human and therefore will never become perfect but this compass will tell us when we have gone off course so that we can get back into the right course again.

"Absolute standards of honesty, purity, unselfishness and love are not goals to be reached, they are a navigational system to steer by. Today long-range rockets use the stars for navigation. Inter-continental rockets use the centre of the earth as a direction finder. But neither the stars nor the centre of the earth is the goal of the voyage. Absolute moral standards show man and humanity when he is off course and how to get back on course. The purpose of moral standards is not perfection, but progress, not sainthood but a society that works." Dr Paul Campbell.

Explain how absolute moral standards show a man when he is off course.

CHARTER FOR SCHOOLS

This "Charter for Schools" was written by a group of young Indians. They decided that the destination of their journey was going to be a new country and a new world. They have put down how each point of the compass will help them to keep to their chosen course.

ABSOLUTE HONESTY IS THE ANSWER TO CORRUPTION. Cheating in schools leads to cheating in business and government. You are of help to your country not because of your virtue and wisdom but because you honestly admit the wrong things you do and change the way you live.

ABSOLUTE PURITY IS THE ANSWER TO BROKEN HOMES AND THE POPULATION EXPLOSION. Character is what you do in the dark. Your decision plus God's help can give you purity. Do you use your time day-dreaming, reading dirty books, or trying to attract attention to yourself? Or are you concerned with helping the people around you to live straight and give their best to nations?

ABSOLUTE UNSELFISHNESS IS THE ANSWER TO POVERTY. There is enough in the world for everyone's need, but not for everyone's greed. If everyone cares enough and everyone shares enough, then everyone will have enough.

ABSOLUTE LOVE IS THE ANSWER TO HATE AND VIOLENCE THAT TEARS A NATION AND THE WORLD APART. The person you are jealous of or hate needs your friendship and help most. Your honest apology to the person you are jealous of or hate can be the starting point of the nation's unity. Love is not dependent on the way other people treat you but the way you treat them.

GOD HAS A PLAN FOR EVERY BOY AND GIRL, MAN AND WOMAN. He has a plan for you. You can find it out. In every heart two voices speak, a good one and a bad one. Take time every morning to kick out the bad one and listen to the good one. Write down the thoughts you get about how to change yourself, others, your home and your country. That will show what your country can do for the world.

QUIZ

What would happen in your nation if more and more people began to judge their actions by these standards?

(a) Would money be saved? How?
(b) Would family rows be fewer? Why?
(c) Would frustration become less? Why?
(d) Would time and energy be saved and used more constructively? Why? How?
(e) Would the country become cleaner? Why?

ACTIVITIES

1. Each student could draw a compass with the four points labelled like this:

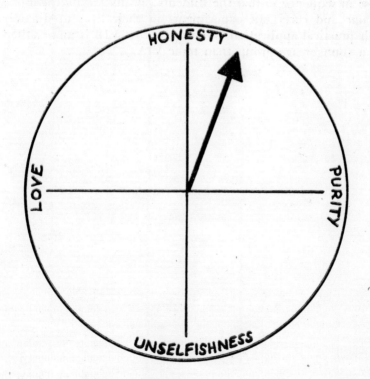

They could keep this on their desks as a reminder of where they are going and how. After some time the class could share experiences of how this compass has brought them back on course. Short plays could be written about these experiences.

2. Posters could be made showing the necessity for absolute standards and what happens if you don't have them.

3. The students could copy out the "Charter for Schools" in large letters to display it. They might have ideas of their own which would relate to their specific situation.

Note

In topics V, VIA, VIB, VII and VIII we go more fully into the meaning and relevance of each of the moral standards mentioned in this topic. We suggest that the teacher goes through these in sequence so that the students can investigate them one by one and carry out experiments in their lives to discover their practical application. We suggest that VIB is more suited for a younger age group than topic VIA.

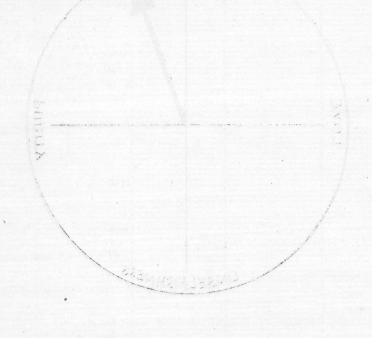

Beyond corruption

AIM

To understand the importance of honesty and integrity. To decide to make it normal in our lives so that we can expect it of others.

DEVELOPMENT

QUIZ

The students should number a paper from 1-7 then write (a), (b) or (c) by the number as the teacher reads the questions, not giving much time for people to think of the answer. They should give the *honest* answer — what they would really do — which is not necessarily the *right* answer.

1. When you do not know the answers in a test do you cheat:
   (a) sometimes?   (b) always?   (c) never?

2. When you are accused of doing something wrong of which you know you are guilty, do you:
   (a) make an excuse?   (b) Deny it?
   (c) Admit it and take the punishment?

3. When you have done something of which you know your parents would not approve, do you:
   (a) Make up a story telling them you have done something they would like you to do?
   (b) Keep quiet and say nothing so as not to hurt them?
   (c) Tell them exactly what you have done and why?

4. If you have already accepted an invitation to go out and

another more interesting alternative is offered, do you:
(a) Go to the first place anyway?
(b) Not turn up at the first place and go to the more interesting occasion?
(c) Tell your first friend some lie to get out of it?

5. If friends ask for help on homework, do you:
(a) Give your work to them to copy?
(b) Explain the work as best you can so that they understand and do it themselves?
(c) Say, "No"?

6. If you have borrowed a pencil or rubber from a friend and several days later you discover you still have it, do you:
(a) Keep it, hoping the friend has forgotten?
(b) Return it with an apology?
(c) Return it when your friend is not there?

7. If the change you are given in a shop is too much, do you:
(a) Take it back immediately?
(b) Keep it and tell your friends how clever you've been?
(c) Keep it, telling yourself that they have probably charged you too much anyway?

Answers: 1. c; 2. c; 3. c; 4. a; 5. b; 6. b; 7. a.

RESULTS

We have experienced that it is best to ask the class how many they have "right" before giving them the following assessment:

If you have 7 correct you are either very dishonest or a saint; 3-6, you are fairly honest with room for improvement! o-3, you are very honest and know exactly where your change can start!

Having given the assessment it has been found worthwhile to go over the quiz questions again to see if the students have any alternative actions to take in these situations. Also they may find it helpful to discuss what would be the right course of action and what prevents them from taking it sometimes. Decisions may follow from the questions raised and new standards of honesty set in the class as a result.

CAN A PERSON BE HONEST AND SURVIVE?

Here are some examples of what people have done to prove that it is possible.

A dealer in automobile spare parts sold Indian-made goods in "Made in USA" boxes at five times the price. He made up his mind to try out honesty. Business actually improved!

His biggest customer had long suspected something and felt he could trust the dealer when he was honest.

A housewife relates her experience of buying a flat.

"We were told that it was impossible to buy a flat without black money. I felt that we should not pay black money. Not everybody is corrupt. There are sound people, you just have to find them. Having hunted quite a bit we were shown one day a flat that was better than all those we had seen before and the price too was lower than that of the others. So we negotiated for it. We were asked for a small amount of black money, but we said no, we were not interested if any black money was involved. Then they just let us have it! It was as simple as that!

"People who have money get impatient. Rather than take a bit of trouble, they give the bribe that is asked for to get their work done. Such people naturally encourage corruption."

The following is a letter from an Indian living at present in Kenya, Africa.

"Men and women all over the world are torn by the need to answer corruption. 'Can I as an individual do anything about it?' and 'It is too big a job and only the government can tackle it' are the sort of questions and attitudes it provokes.

"I have an experience to relate.

"Some weeks ago I was cornered into a situation where a bribe seemed the only way out. And many of us, some more than once, have landed in such situations.

"I believe that 'When man listens God speaks. When man obeys, God acts and when men change nations change.' In a few moments of quiet, the thought came to me, 'Have vision and really believe that these three men with whom you are dealing can be builders of a new Kenya and a new world free of hate, fear, greed, bullying and corruption.' I then told them what a rascal I'd been and the challenge which made me decide to be different.

"I described how as a student I had decided to return 'permanently borrowed' library books. How I had hated a particular race but later apologised for my hatred. How as a student secretary in a hostel I had pilfered money from the students' fund while at the same time attacking corruption from university platforms, and paid the money back. How I bribed a customs officer in a certain port and smuggled goods into the country without paying duty and how later I went and apologised and paid up the duty. I told them I did this because that was the price to be paid for creating a new society. I told them that they could do it too.

"The three men quickly sensed a challenge, not just to stop being corrupt themselves, but so to live that they actually became part of the cure. They left with a warm handshake."

A medical student from Bombay says, "When I measured my life by the standard of absolute honesty I found I was just as corrupt as the people I had learnt to blame. I commute ten miles to and from college every day. The rush-hour crush gives every commuter ample opportunity to bewail his plight and spew vengeance upon the railways. But did I have a right to criticise when I sometimes travelled without a ticket? I decided to wage war with my weakness, which had held me captive for years, by restoring to the railways the sum I owed them.

"When I approached the railways I was shunted from station to station till I finally arrived at the office of the Deputy Commercial Superintendent. When I announced my decision to him he was most surprised. A few days later I read a news agency report of my story. I know of three national newspapers that have carried it."

DISCUSSION TOPICS

1. Read again the last paragraph of the story about the house-wife. What is black money? Why do so many people use it? Do you agree with what the housewife says? What can each one of us do about this sort of thing?

2. The Indian living in Kenya asked himself, "Can I as an individual do anything about corruption?" What did he do

and how did it affect the others? Are there similar things
that each one of you can do?

3. What the medical student did reached the newspapers.
What made it a news story? Does doing something because
everyone else does it, make it right? Why did this student
make restitution? Are there things which you can put right
which will free you from being a "captive" of your
weakness?

DEBATE TOPICS

(a) Where there is no truth there is no trust.
(b) Love without honesty is sentimentality; honesty without
love is brutality.

ACTIVITIES

The class could dramatise some of the stories quoted here and/
or could dramatise their own experiences in order to pass on
what they have learnt to others in the school or even in the
community.

Another way of spreading their ideas might be to write
to local newspapers as did the man from Kenya. It is important
that they decide to live honestly not for the sake of becoming
good, but in order to bring a change in society starting where
they are.

TOPIC VI A
3 to 4 lessons

Purity — the source of true freedom

AIM

1. To understand that living purity is not only a personal matter, but a national need.
2. Purity of thought, motive and action frees the individual to be creative and to have the energy and the selflessness to tackle some of the vast problems of the world.

DEVELOPMENT

Ask the class to make two lists — the first one of things which they consider to be beautiful and the second of anything they consider to be ugly. Make a list on the board from their suggestions. Examine with them what makes certain things beautiful and other things ugly in their minds. Has it anything to do with certain things being clean and others dirty? Is it only a matter of opinion or are there some suggestions on which the whole class is agreed? Is it man-made things or those of God's creation which feature most in the list of beautiful things? Why is this so? Is there something in the human heart which responds to the perfect?

One often reads on products one buys, "*Pure* vegetable oil", "*100%* cotton", "*Pure* gold" and so on. What is meant by "pure" and "100%" in these instances? Can you think of other examples?

1. What is meant by being pure of heart and mind?
   The Upanishads say: "Let one therefore keep his mind pure, for what a man thinks he becomes."

2. What are the elements which contaminate one's heart?
3. What is being used to pollute people's minds?
4. What do these contaminating and polluting elements do to us?

The students may like to write down their answers to the above questions. A young Swedish girl writes of her experience of what living with a pure heart and mind means to her. Give this to the class to consider and discuss.

"Purity gives you a sparkle and gaiety that do not have to be put on. It satisfies you deep down and I believe it is the normal way to live. Permissiveness (always doing what you want, when you want to do it) instead of satisfying, just makes you grab more and more."

Let the class compare this with their own experience. Have they found this to be true?

She goes on to say, "What do you do when temptation comes? I find I can do one of three things. I can give up and fail. I can try and fight it in my own strength. Or I can turn to God and win the struggle. When I do that, He always tells me to open my heart wider and wider and to think for more and more people. Purity and care for others go together in my life, and that is why I think it is progressive."

Note

At this stage we recommend that the teacher follows through the point about temptation. In the topic entitled "Keeping on the right path" this matter is dealt with in more detail. It was put in at the request of several students.

Our nation, to be strong, must be clean and united. This means that the people in it must be clean, not only outside, but inside too.

5. How can we rid ourselves of the impure elements in our hearts and minds?

A Burmese educator, Daw Nyein Tha, used to give this illustration:

Your heart is meant to be like a pool of water — cool, clear and sparkling. Everyone who comes to drink of it goes away refreshed. Then a leaf falls and goes down to the bottom and then another and another. They all go down to the bottom. When you look at the pond, the water looks clear, but stir it up and all the leaves come up. You cannot drink it any more.

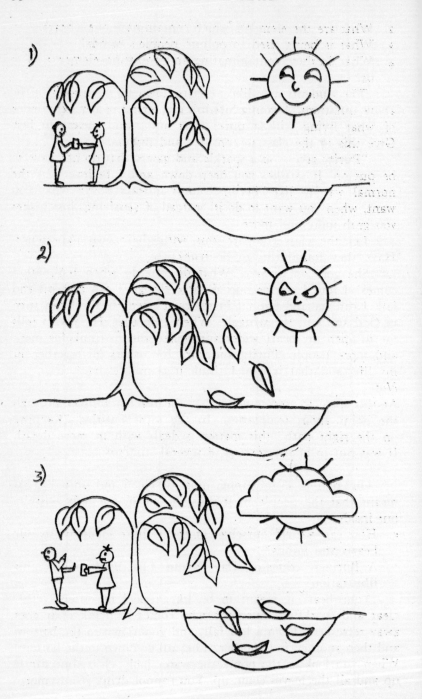

The only thing to do to have it clean again is to get all the
water and dirt out, clean the whole pond and then put in fresh
water. To keep it clean, you have to take the leaves out one
by one as they fall, but now it is easier because the water is
clean and each new leaf can be seen. (One leaf may be jealousy
of a friend, or telling a lie etc.) Take it out, recognise it for
what it is and then throw it away. The pool remains clear, cool
and sparkling. Anyone can drink from it and go away with
new life. When your heart is pure like the pool, you can bring
happiness and help to those around you.

ACTIVITY

Ask the class to draw an illustration of this story, writing on
the leaves the elements they have each recognised as the ones
which most contaminate their hearts and pollute their minds,
and which they have decided to throw out whenever they
appear.

The following are the words of a song. The music can
be found on page 147. It is another illustration of the need
for a pure heart.

Water For A Thirsty Land

Chorus
Water for a thirsty land,
Cool water, cool water,
Who'll bring water for a thirsty land,
Water for a thirsty land?

1. The world is like a desert
Where the land is parched and dry,
And people burn with a thirst for things
Which just don't satisfy.

2. And millions drink from the rivers of hate,
Which seem so swift and sure,
They burn with a mighty passion
That can never bring a cure.

3. There is a stream of water
That can fill and satisfy.
It comes to you as you give it away,
And it never, never runs dry.

4. I've counted all my treasures,
And the things I long to do,
I'll gladly give the best I have
Till the world has a purpose new.

A MATTER OF NATIONAL IMPORTANCE

Discuss the following points with the students:

Deciding to have absolute purity as a standard in our lives is
not only a personal matter. It can be important nationally
and internationally. If one studies the earlier empires and the
reasons why they became weak and were eventually destroyed,
one can see that the start of their fall was the increased
immorality of their citizens, e.g. the Roman and the Athenian
Empires. Impurity saps the strength of a nation. It takes away
the clarity of vision and the unselfishness of motive.

Examine what is happening in the more affluent nations
of the world. In Sweden, the suicide rate is the highest in the
world. In America, violence in the streets of the large cities has
increased alarmingly in recent years. In Japan, pollution is
one of its greatest problems.

Are these signs of health and happiness? These are the
fruits of societies where people have given in to self-indulgence.

The following figures indicate the trend in Britain as her
society has become more affluent and more permissive:

Offences as the result of drink increased between 1969
and 1974 by 47%.

During the same period the number of patients admitted
to mental hospitals as a result of alcohol-based problems
increased by over 50%.

Serious crimes (including murder, violence, robbery,
forgery and blackmail) have doubled in the last ten
years.

Robberies in the streets have doubled in the last four
years.

Attacks on the police have increased 186% in the last four
years.

Vandalism and arson are costing local education authorities
over £15 million a year.

Abortions for girls under nineteen years of age in 1973
were three times the number in 1969.

Dr J. D. Unwin made a study of the world's principal
civilisations and of eighty uncivilised societies. His findings
were set out in his book *Sex and Culture* and these words
from that book summarise his findings: "Any human society

is free to choose either to display great energy or to enjoy sexual freedom; the evidence is that it cannot do both for more than one generation."[1]

PROJECT WORK

Older students may like to do a project to discover more facts on what is happening in different countries now.

Others may have an interest in history and could investigate for themselves the point about the root of destruction of an empire being the increased immorality of the citizens.

Yet others may like to find out what has been the inspiration of the great art, drama and dance of their country.

Here is an account of what was done by a class of twelve-year-olds in a school in Beirut, Lebanon. It is the sort of action to which our personal decisions should lead us. When we are freed from our self-concern we can see better what needs to be done to improve things around us.

PROTECT OUR PLANET

"I think we should do something about it." The words were from Ali, a twelve-year-old boy in a Social Studies class. The question under discussion was that of the world-wide pollution of the environment.

"What would you suggest?" he was asked. "Clean up the playing fields after school today," he replied.

That afternoon the teacher and three of the boys went ahead with the task and deposited the rubbish in the largely unused bins at the gates.

The next week more boys joined in but this time by-standers began shouting, "Garbage pickers! Garbage pickers." People in that part of the world have an abhorrence towards "menial work", but the boys had not expected this assault.

The teacher of the class had long believed that God could direct in minor and major decisions in life. Therefore there had been a practice of having a minute's silence before the start of every lesson, after which anyone could tell the class what ideas he had had.

The morning after the group clean-up the teacher's

[1] For more details and statistics see Resource Material (page 65) and the Bibliography.

thought was that they should not be discouraged by the mis-
understanding of their aim by others. Ali's contribution was,
"Let us start a club, open to the whole school, where we not
only clean up the campus, but also plant some trees and
flowers."

"What shall we call it?" someone asked. "Protect our
Planet," was the inspired reply. "P.O.P. Club."

They selected a patch on which to start a garden but as
they knew nothing about gardening a delegation went to the
wife of the president of the nearby university to ask for her
help. She willingly came and advised them what to do.

One day the teacher had the thought, "We shall only get
the world cleaned up if each one of us is willing to do what
we want others to do." For him it meant picking up rubbish
dropped along the corridors and on the pathways between
the buildings. He began to do this ostentatiously, to the
amusement of the pupils and the amazement of the other
teachers. Some of the boys began to join him. They began to
be greeted with the cry, "Pop Club! Pop Club!" But ridicule
turned to imitation and that year the school was noticeably
cleaner.

The outreach towards the big world problems was, however, still limited to the school body. But one boy kept bringing
up a proposal to prepare a petition. This was eventually agreed
to and read.

"We, the undersigned, young and older citizens and
residents of Mid-Eastern countries pledge ourselves to
protect our natural environment, air, water, land, trees,
flowers, birds and wild animals against destruction, pollution and waste. This we do for our own enjoyment and
for the benefit of all other countries and of the generations
to come.

"We petition all youth in our countries, and the adults in
politics, labour, business and the professions to join with
us in protecting the future of our planet."

A CHAIN OF EVENTS WAS STARTED

The school director authorised 1,000 copies to be mimeo-
graphed and over 800 signatures were collected in the school.
A neighbouring school caught the idea and joined in. A professor connected with UNESCO and the discussions on con-

servation, saw the petition and had it displayed in the lobby of the hall where 1,000 delegates were meeting on this subject. He also invited Ali to address these representatives in their closing session. In thanking him, he said, "We have not sufficiently considered the contribution youth can make."

The Women's League in the capital city heard about the Pop Club and invited six members to speak to their meeting. As a result they announced that their programme for the next year would be based on the principles of the petition and the practices of the Club.

On the last day of the school year the guests, teachers and pupils were walking from the closing assembly beside the completed flower bed, bright with geraniums. Not all of them appreciated its significance, but Ali and his club mates had learned that any one of them could be an agent to whom God gives an idea and that, if they were obedient, a chain of constructive action could begin whose outcome could be far beyond imagination. It may begin at our fingertips.

QUESTIONS

1. Is there anywhere in the school or surroundings where you can start cleaning up?

2. Think out ways in which you can enlist the rest of the school (e.g. the students' own example; explaining at school assembly etc.)

3. The boys in the Lebanon not only cleared up the mess, they also planted flowers. What can you do to make your surroundings more beautiful?

ACTIVITY

The students could make posters for the school corridors to illustrate all these things and to help the rest of the school to think about them. These can be made up of cuttings from newspapers, magazines, etc. as well as drawings.

One school made notices saying "I CARE" at each place where the students needed to think of others, e.g. at a tap which should be turned off after use, or near a rubbish bin into which all the rubbish should be put, rather than left lying on the ground. Your class will have other ideas.

CONCLUSION

There is yet another reason for living disciplined lives. There are times when our nation may be threatened, either from within or from without. It is then that those who have clear consciences are the ones with the moral strength to stand up and fight for what is right. If you have things in your life of which you are ashamed and which you want to hide from others, you then live in fear of being found out.

Have you done anything which you are scared that others will find out? Can you free yourself from that fear? How?

Suggest that the class takes time to sit in silence and let their Inner Voice speak to them on these questions.

Many people have found a new freedom when they have been able to be honest about these things.

Discuss with the class the following statements:

1. It is a fact that SIN blinds, binds, deafens and deadens the heart.
2. SIN has the big "I" in the middle. When that is crossed out and God's will is chosen, then true freedom has been found.
3. The happiest and most creative people are those with a clear conscience.

RESOURCE MATERIAL

The New Morality and *The Cult of Softness,* two books by Arnold Lunn and Garth Lean, give more detail of J. D. Unwin's work and findings. The following are some quotations given in these two books on the relation between national energy and moral standards.

Unwin writing about the Hellenes:

"These absolutely monogamous men displayed great expansive energy.... They were deistic, monarchical and extremely energetic. ... By the end of the fifth century, however, the old customs had disappeared, the sexual opportunities of both the sexes being extended. There was no compulsory continence; sexual desires could be satisfied in the most direct manner. ... The energy of the Athenians declined. Three generations later the once vigorous city, torn by dissension, was subject to a foreign master."

W. E. H. Lecky writes of the declining years of the Roman

Republic: "The Roman religion established the sanctity of
an oath ... it sustained the supremacy of the father in the
family, surrounded marriage with many imposing solemnities.
... It strengthened some of the best habits of the people. But
these habits and the religious reverence with which they were
connected soon disappeared amid the immorality and de-
composition that marked the closing years of the Republic. ...
The complete subversion of the social and political system of
the Republic, the anarchy of civil war, the ever increasing
concourse of strangers, bringing with them new philosophies,
customs and gods had dissolved or effaced all the old bonds of
virtue."

Professor Pitirim Sorokin writes about the Russian experiment: "During the first stage of the Revolution, its
leaders deliberately attempted to destroy marriage and the
family. Free love was glorified. ... The legal distinction between
marriage and casual sexual intercourse was abolished. ... One
could marry and divorce as many times as desired. ... Within
a few years, hordes of wild, homeless children became a real
menace to the Soviet Union itself. Millions of lives, especially
of young girls were wrecked; divorces skyrocketed, as also did
abortions. The hatreds and conflicts among polygamous and
polyandrous mates rapidly mounted and so did psychoneuroses.
Work in the nationalised factories slackened. The total
results were so appalling that the government was forced to
reverse its policy.....its place was taken by official glorification
of premarital chastity and of the sanctity of marriage. ... Soviet
Russia today has a more monogamic, stable and Victorian
family and marriage life than do most of the Western
countries."

Friendship

AIMS

To learn that real friendship is based on giving rather than getting.

DEVELOPMENT

Give the class the following questionnaire, the answers to be written down.

1. Do I only like the people who like me?
2. What sort of people do I want to have as my friends?
3. Why are there some people with whom I do not want to be friends?
4. Is it an inevitable fact that there will always be some people whom I don't want as my friends?
5. Why do I *want* friends? Why do I *need* friends?
6. How do I react when my friends tell me the truth about myself?
7. Am I ready to risk my friendship with anyone in order to say something or do something which I know to be right?
8. Do I feel jealous when my friends do better than I do in class, sports etc?
9. What do you think is true friendship?
10. What are the things which break friendship?

Collect in these answers which need not have their names on them. Divide the class into groups and get each group to discuss one of the following problems. If the class is not used

to group discussions, they may need some help in how to
conduct them. Get each group to choose a leader of the discussion and also someone who will record the main conclusions
and be able to report back to the rest of the class.

DISCUSSION PROBLEMS

1. Sunita and Rekha are good friends. One morning, in the
   middle of the exams, Rekha comes to school and tells Sunita
   that she was sick last evening and was unable to revise
   for the exams. She asks Sunita to help her cheat. What
   should Sunita do?
2. Someone in the class has spilt ink over a book on the teacher's
   desk. The teacher has asked who has done it, but no one
   has owned up. Vijayalakshmi knows her friend has done
   it. Should she tell the teacher or what should she do?
3. Radha's mother does not like the friends with whom her
   daughter mixes. She feels that they lead Radha into
   trouble. Radha says she has the right to choose her own
   friends. What do you think?
4. Jyoti and Mangala are good friends. Yet Jyoti often criticises
   her friend when she is not there. If Jyoti were saying these
   things to you, what would you do?
5. You are playing with some of your friends. A girl from
   another class comes up and asks if she can join you. Some
   of your friends say, "No. We've got enough people." You
   know this isn't true. It is because they do not want a girl
   from another class. Do you think you should say something
   in this situation or should you stay quiet? Give the reasons
   for the course of action you take.

Use the answers from the questionnaire and the results
of these discussions to draw out in the next lesson the main
points about friendship.

The following points are important ones to be made,
but it is best if they can be given by the students, as you
discuss the questionnaire answers and results of the discussion
groups.

1. True friendship is only built if there is an attitude of giving
   rather than of getting.
2. Honesty is the key to friendship as it creates the trust
   which is essential for friendship to last.

3. Friendships should not be exclusive. No one should feel left out. If they do, then the friendship is a selfish one.

4. Our friendships often have ourselves in the centre of them. We can tell this if the people we choose as friends are those whom we can dominate or order around. Also this is true if we feel jealous when our friends do better than we do.

5. We can be friends with everyone if we want to be. Friendships do not depend solely upon natural affinities. Sometimes the best and most lasting friendships are those which have to be worked at.

6. A wife once said to her husband, "I will love you as you are, but I will fight for you to become what you are meant to be." The aim of friendship should be to help the other person to be the best sort of person he can be. This is why we need our friends.

7. Friends who stop us from doing the things we know to be right, are not true friends.

Friendship is like a triangle. Draw one, as below:

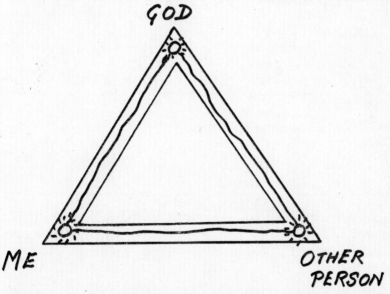

This relationship is like an electric current flowing around the triangle. It only works if the connection is unbroken. If there is something wrong between you and the other person (what things could these be?) then your contact with God is broken. If there is something which your conscience tells you is between you and God, what will happen between you and the other person? Does a small gap cut the power just as much as a big one?

Suggest that after all this discussion all the students spend a few minutes in silence to consider the following questions:

"Is there anything wrong between myself and anyone else which is blocking my friendship with them, especially in this class? If so, what can I do about it? When will I do it?"

When adequate time has been given for the students to write down their answers, give them a chance to tell what they have discovered and even carry out the thoughts then and there. If some have the thought to apologise to someone not in the class then make sure that one of his/her friends takes on to see that the thought is carried out.

ACTIVITIES

Get the students to find stories which show the value of true friendship. The *Reader's Digest* is a good source of such stories.

Keeping on the right path

AIMS

To learn how to make it normal to overcome temptation. To discover the power whereby we can do this.

DEVELOPMENT

Do you ever find yourself doing things which you know are wrong? What was the last occasion on which you did it and what did you do? (Get the class to write it down.) Also write down the answer to why you did it. (The class should not feel obliged to tell what they have written.)

All of us, however young or old we are, sometimes find ourselves in situations like this. We find ourselves tempted to do wrong things. Temptation is a normal thing which happens in life. The question is, what do we do about it? It is only wrong if we give in to it.

A man once said, "We cannot prevent the birds from flying over our heads, but we can stop them from nesting in our hair." What do you think he meant by this?

The progression from temptation to doing the wrong thing is usually — the look, the thought, the fascination and the fall. Ask each member of the class to draw this progression in their books by means of illustrations, e.g. a girl sees a nice pen sitting on her neighbour's desk. She's alone in the room at that moment. The thought comes into her mind that she would like the pen. The thought and the desire grow stronger and stronger, until she finally gives in and takes the pen.

Where do you think is the easiest place to stop this train of events?

THE CAMEL AND THE TENT

Put the drawings on the board, or have them already drawn on large sheets of paper.

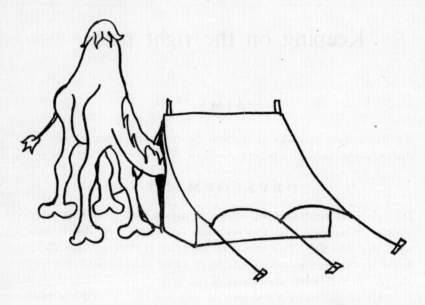

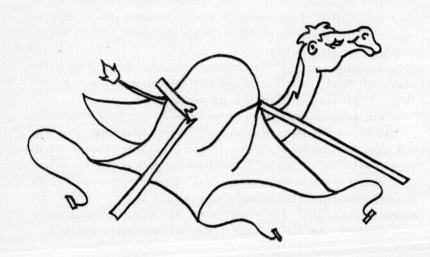

Ask the class the following questions:

First Picture:
1. What is this? (point to the tent)
2. What is the animal?
3. What is he trying to do?
4. Does he belong in there?
5. Then why is he trying to get in? (to make mischief)
6. How do you suggest we can get him out?
7. Would it be any use just saying in a gentle voice, "Please camel go outside"? (No, we have to be drastic and very firm.)
8. When is it easier to get him out? When he has only his head in or when he is completely inside?

There is an Arab proverb which says, "The whole camel does not have to get into the tent, only its nose and you know it is there by the smell."

Second Picture:
This is what happens when we let the camel in. Get the class to say what has happened. (Everything collapses and there is no room for anything else.)

Now let's see what we have learnt about temptation. Imagine that the tent is your heart and the camel is temptation. Go through the questions 3-8, above.

Turn to the second picture and the total collapse. This is what happens when we give in to temptation. Often it puts us in a mood.

1. What is a mood?
2. Do your moods affect other people?
3. Do other peoples' moods affect you?
4. What do day-dreams and dirty thoughts do to you? Do they:
   a. Help you to care for others?
   b. Make you think more of yourself?
5. If you have things in your life that you want to hide, what effect does this have on you and your attitude to other people?
6. When do you have most temptations?
   a. When you are busy with lots of things to occupy yourself?
   b. When you are bored or unhappy?

7. What is the best way you know of getting out of a mood?

Someone once said that the faster a car goes the less the mud sticks to the wheels. We are the same. It is when we are going very slowly that the bad voice inside us has the best chance of getting us stuck in the mud.

Ask the class to write down the things which they get tempted by — the situations which make you do wrong things — how can they be avoided?

EXAMPLES

If your problem is falling off cliffs, why walk along the edge of them? e.g. If certain people don't help you to do the right things, then don't mix with them. If reading certain kinds of books makes you have dirty thoughts, then do not read them, etc.

Note

When one class was discussing this question, a girl admitted that she had a daily temptation to take biscuits out of the biscuit tin at home, which meant there was never enough for the rest of the family. She asked for suggestions as to how she could deal with this. Her friends came up with several ideas, ranging from telling her mother to hide the tin, to not going into the room where the tin was and even telling her brothers and sister that this was a temptation and asking them to help her not to do it.

The main point of encouraging the students to air these problems is to encourage them to help each other overcome the weaknesses in their character so that they have the practical experience of change in their lives. It is these experiences which will give them the hope that other, larger problems in their lives can be solved.

Temptations do not like the light of day. What is it that keeps us quiet about our temptations? If we bring them out into the open their power usually lessens. Even if we fall down into the mud, we do not have to stay there. We can tell someone we trust, decide never to do it again and ask God's help in this. Fortunately, the Power which made us, with all our instincts and desires gives us the ability to control them. During the next week make an experiment of doing this every time you are tempted to do something wrong and see if it helps. (At the end of the week some of the class may like to say what the results have been.)

We need to have big enough reasons for not giving in to temptations. Sometimes, for example, we find ourselves telling lies in order to get ourselves out of trouble. If we are only thinking about ourselves, that is the most reasonable thing to do. However, if we want to find an answer to the corruption in our country, then we will not do it.

What reasons would make you want to live the way you know you should?

The students gave answers to questions at the very beginning of this topic. Now encourage them to see, in the light of what they have learnt, what they can do about them.

To lead is to serve

AIMS

To enlist the students in taking moral leadership and responsibility, whoever they are. Also to recognise that the quality of unselfishness is what gives real strength to a leader.

DEVELOPMENT

Think of those who are the leaders in your class and in the school. What sort of people do we usually choose as leaders?
1. People who want the power and recognition that comes from that position?
2. People who are out to help others?

   If we want to become leaders who are respected by our followers, we need to live a quality of life which they can respect. The most difficult place to serve unselfishly is at home. Let the students ask themselves the following questions and answer them honestly:

1. Do I take for granted what is done for me at home? What should I do?
2. If there is any work to be done at home do I offer or quietly sit hoping someone else will offer?
3. Do I ever make an excuse of doing homework when I could offer to help?
4. Do I ever think of doing something for another member of any family which would surprise and please them? How do I feel when I have done it?
5. When a fight starts at home is it ever because of my selfishness?

6. Do I make a fuss about food? If so why?
7. Do I get angry when my will is crossed? Why?
8. If every member started thinking this way what sort of family would I have?
9. Can I expect others to start if I do not set an example? If not, then where can I start and how?

It would be an interesting experiment for each student to put into action the answer they have given to question number 9. Next week they can tell the class how they have got on.

Note
One student who tried the experiment of applying the standard of absolute unselfishness over a week-end, said firmly on the Monday morning, "It doesn't work!" On being questioned further he replied, "I helped Mum with her shopping, I cleaned Dad's shoes and even helped my sister but I didn't get one word of appreciation." One of his fellow students immediately stated, "That's not absolute unselfishness. You were hoping to get something out of it."

Encourage the class to do some research to find out those people who have served the nation selflessly. What have they achieved? (e.g. Mother Teresa). These people have not necessarily taken political leadership but in their own way they have led people to do what is needed.

Can the students now think of any men and women who died a short or a long time ago who were such great leaders of their people that many still follow their ideas and way of life now? Who? How did they live? Were they basically selfish or unselfish in their motives?

There can be both good and bad leaders. Give examples of bad leaders in the past. Why were they bad? Were they selfish or unselfish in what they did? In spite of these things, why did people follow them?

There are also certain forces which corrupt and spoil good leaders. What are they? Let the class suggest what they think first and then add any of the following if they have not been mentioned — selfish ambition, power, lust for position and status, greed, love of the limelight, flattery etc.

Leaders have to make many decisions. On what can they base these decisions? One useful maxim is that it is *"what is right not who is right"* that matters. An example of how one

member of the Sudanese government gave this sort of leadership will be found under Resource Material (page 82).

The class should make a list of the qualities they believe
make the sort of leader they would gladly follow. (See under
Resource Material Field Marshal Manekshaw's points of leadership, which may be worth discussing when the students have
written their own lists.)

DISCUSSION TOPICS

Divide the class into small groups of not more than ten to
fifteen. Let each group discuss one of the following topics after
which they can share their findings with the rest of the class.

1. Are leaders born or made? Can anyone become a leader?
   Can one decide to become a leader or does one have to
   be chosen?
2. To have leaders there must be followers. Do followers have
   any responsibility for the sort of leader they have? Should
   they follow blindly — without questioning — what their
   leader says or does? What should they do?
3. Does flattering a leader help him or her? What does it do?
   Why do followers flatter? How can followers help their
   leader most?
4. Does the state of a nation depend most upon the quality
   of her leaders or the quality of her ordinary citizens, or
   is it a responsibility which must be carried by both? Give
   reasons for your answer.

Note

While the discussions are in progress the teacher should
unobtrusively watch the groups and see how the leaders of the
groups are conducting themselves. Has anyone taken over the
discussion? Are they drawing out ideas from everyone in an
unselfish manner? etc. Afterwards the teacher can mention
these points and find out from the students how the leaders
were chosen. Were they chosen by the group or self-appointed?
Having become leaders, did they take charge or help people to
come to the point? Questions like these can help to bring out
the qualities needed in a leader.

STUDENT PROJECT

How does all this apply to me? Ask the following questions of six people in your school, preferably not in your class:

1. What career do you want to have when you leave school?
2. Is your main aim to make as much money as possible?
3. What will you do with the money you earn?
4. Do you have any other reason for choosing that career? If so, what is it?
5. Will your attitude help to answer the problems of the country?
6. Would you choose a different career if you were doing it from an unselfish motive?

Now examine the answers you have been given, and consider the following:

How do people usually choose a career?
Are these reasons mostly selfish or unselfish?
If *you* were being absolutely unselfish and thinking of your nation and what the world needs most, what would you use your life to do?
Which career would help you to do this, taking into account the things you can do best?
In what professions do people serve the community most?
Draw up a questionnaire to ask one or two people already serving in the professions you have mentioned.
Ask them questions which will tell you why they are doing what they are and how they made their choice in the first place.
Compare these answers with the ones you received from people in the school. While doing this, consider the following:

1. Is serving the community an attitude of mind, or does it depend on one's job?
2. Can one only take responsibility if one has an important position?
3. With what attitude will I enter my career?
4. What points will I now consider in choosing my career?

ACTIVITIES

DEBATE

"This house believes that to lead is to serve."

Have speakers for and against this motion and then take a vote in the class.

DISCUSSION TOPIC

A man who was fighting for civil liberties on behalf of a minority once said, "No one can take away from me the right to be responsible." A man or woman who takes responsibility often finds him/herself in a position of leadership. Discuss.

ESSAY OR PLAY

Write an essay or a play about one of the people who has served humanity selflessly. Do it in such a way that it will challenge and inspire others to think through what they use their lives for in the future. Use what you have written so that other people have the chance to read or see it.

RESOURCE MATERIAL

SIX ATTRIBUTES OF LEADERSHIP

Extracts from an article by Field-Marshall Sam Manekshaw in "Himmat", 19 July 1974.

There is one school of thought which insists that leaders are born. I do not agree with this theory. I submit to you that we can make leaders. ... To my way of thinking there are certain attributes which are essential to leadership. All of these can be cultivated. What are these?

1. *Professional knowledge and competence* are the *sine qua non* without which there would only be pretence at being a leader. No one is born with professional knowledge and competence. It has to be acquired the hard way. One has to study one's profession continuously and throughout one's life.

2. *Taking a decision.* Next in order of priority is the ability to take a decision and ensure that the decision is complied with. ... An act of omission is as dangerous as an act of

commission. ... "To do nothing is to do something which is definitely wrong."

3. *Absolute justice and impartiality.* You can never obtain the respect of your men unless you are absolutely just and impartial; and without the respect of your men you can never lead them. No man likes being superseded; and yet men will accept punishment stoically no matter how severe it is, provided that they know that no matter what the status of the individual, all will be treated alike.

4. *Moral courage* ... It is the ability to distinguish right from wrong and, having so distinguished it, to be prepared to say so, irrespective of the views held by your superiors or subordinates and of consequences to yourself. No "yes man" will ever make a leader ... as he will be despised in equal measure, by those who have elevated him, by his colleagues and by his subordinates.

5. *Physical courage.* Fear is a natural phenomenon, and no man is free from it. ... Being frightened is one thing and showing fear is quite another. It is when your knees are knocking and your teeth are chattering that it is essential to show your physical courage and assert your leadership. ... If men see their superior frightened they will lose all respect for him; he might hang on to his job, but he will never again be able to lead them.

6. *The human touch.* It must never be forgotten that you are not dealing with machines but with human beings, and human beings in the mass can be wicked, cruel, corrupt and ill-disciplined. Therefore, a leader must be able to deal with them firmly and quite ruthlessly when these traits become manifest. But he must also never forget that humans have human problems — problems of death, sickness, debt etc. So the leader must have the human touch and the ability to win their confidence ... and he must have a sense of humour to make them laugh when things are not going smoothly. ... Finally a leader must learn one more thing. He must know when to shut up; when the chaps have had enough and won't take any more.

"I HAD TO SET CLEAR GUIDELINES"

Dr Murtada is the Director General of Labour and Employment in the Sudan, whose initiative and commitment has produced the new six-year plan. He talks of how, when in Geneva in 1961, he met people who made him rethink his whole life. "Instead of ambitious political aims and going with the popular tide, I felt then that I had to serve and set clear guidelines for my needy people. 'People first' became the essence of my ideology.

"I decided to start to fight in the Labour Research Department that the proceeds of economic growth would percolate to the poorest strata of the population, not widen the gap and line the pockets of the officials, of those already affluent. This is working out.

"Some of us graduates decided to accept the sacrifice involved. For years I had had none of the status symbols of my rank in the civil service — car, house and so on. I could not demand of others what I was unwilling to do myself. It has meant only taking one week's leave in six years. When on official conferences abroad, I usually pay my postage and transport costs myself as I feel I can afford it better than the average Sudanese taxpayer who would otherwise have to cover it. I chase up bills to be paid rather than accept the bribe implied in delay or non-presentation.

"These things add up and get noticed. Lately, following publication of our national plan, I have had to turn down several offers from multi-national enterprises, the Gulf States and the oil industry. My job was not only to conceive and architect the plan, but also, and this is harder, to serve as midwife in its implementation. There will be battles ahead."

One important feature of the plan is that the south of the country is to be given priority at the expense of the comparatively developed north. In this there is a recognition of past wrongs and a determination towards equity and justice for the southern non-Moslem tribes. It indicates a long-awaited change of heart on the part of the northern, Arab establishment towards their essentially African and Christian or Pagan compatriots in the south.

Murtada's policy looks at the human implications rather than short-term results. It is the poorest section of the community which is being deliberately affected. He and the colleagues he has inspired are ready for opposition from vested interests and are prepared to battle it out, for the wider sake of neighbouring nations in strife for whom the Sudanese experiment in reconciliation forms a focus of hope.

Can the world be fed ?

AIMS

To investigate in some detail the problems of the world's food supply and the quality of unselfishness necessary in our lives to bring lasting solutions.

DEVELOPMENT

Find out what is the world food situation.
Why is it that enough food is not being produced?
Is it possible to produce more food?
Does the present situation have to continue or is there an answer?

The following passage from a speech made in May 1975 in India may be of help to study. It was by Mr S. F. Barnes M.B.E., for a number of years the Project Manager for the Australian Dairy Board in S. E. Asia.

"In recent years the whole question of world food supplies has become prominent. Why? If we go back to the early 1960s it was a period of surplus food. Then, almost dramatically, in the early 1970s there was a world food shortage. The reason is that with increasing costs in the West, with increasing surpluses which could not be disposed of, there was a tendency to restrict production. At the same time, the population was increasing across the world. Then in 1972 there was a series of major droughts and floods in many countries. Suddenly the world realised that the reserves of food had dwindled from stocks enough to feed the world for some ninety days to enough to feed the world for only twenty days.

"Immediately after the troubles of 1972 we had the increase in the oil prices and the rapid increases of costs in the West, with inflation. Food which was cheap in the 1960s suddenly became expensive. Milk powder which used to be sold for 200 dollars a ton in 1964-1965, rocketed up to over 1,000 dollars a ton. In this situation, governments restricted production and you got a changing pattern in food production in the West.

"In an age of technological development, this is a very serious state of affairs. To die of hunger in this age is to be murdered. Yet across the world many people die of hunger.

"What are the other factors? One is that we have lost the compassion to produce what people need. Today we produce not what is needed or even what the market demands. We tend to produce what we can sell at a profit. We are exporting from the West no milk powder today, although in the developing countries, there is extensive malnutrition. In India the medical authorities estimate that 40 million children below the age of six suffer from serious malnutrition. Children with serious malnutrition do not develop properly and cannot have the same intelligence. You cannot make up what is lost in those early years.

"There is the factor of wastage. An estimated 25% of the grain produced in all the developing countries is wasted through poor storage, through rats and other vermin and through damp.

"What is the answer? Firstly in the immediate situation the developing countries such as India cannot produce all the food they really need but the West can. Slowly we are building a force of people in the West who care enough, who have the compassion to see that the food gets to those who need it. This is needed at both ends. I was a delegate to the International Dairy Congress in Delhi last year. Many of us were concerned to ensure that decisions were made to make milk available where it is needed. I found that opposition was coming from some of the Indian delegates who said in effect, 'We don't want your milk powder. You give us money and other assistance and we will produce it ourselves.' I interrupted and said, 'Does this mean that the people in India will have the

same lack of compassion as the people in the West? Are you
not concerned that forty million children are suffering in this
country?' There was a wave of applause across the room.

"We all have to face the fact that unless we deal with our
pride, unless we really learn to care and share, we will not
solve these problems of nutrition.

"What is the position for the future? I believe that India
in the future can produce all the food needed. It will need a
massive amount of help from all over the world. It means that
not only must the West be willing to help, but India and other
countries must be willing to accept help. People overseas must
also be sure that the help given is properly used. I'm sorry
to say that we grab on to a thing like corruption and use it
as an excuse for not helping. People say to me that it will be
used in the wrong places and in the wrong way. This is not
true, but while we have our faults in the West, there are faults
here, too. We are going to have to deal with corruption.

"People say that we can now produce our own milk here
in India. This is true. It is an outstanding example of what
can be done. Unfortunately there is the risk that the milk
produced will be too expensive for people to buy. Milk in
the cities is now so dear that only the people with a high
income can buy it. Although in Australia and New Zealand
we have high standards of living and high costs, we can produce
milk cheaper than you can produce it in India. The reason is
that our countries are natural milk producing countries and
these are not. Therefore the answer does not always lie in
doing it yourself. The answer lies in the whole world allocating
production where it can be done most cheaply in the interests
of the people.

"The grinding poverty and hopelessness of many people
in the developing countries will only be overcome by a new
spirit of care, unselfishness and responsible co-operation on the
part of all."

QUESTIONS

1. Why have the countries of the West restricted their food
   production?
2. "To die of hunger in this age is to be murdered." What do
   you think this means?

3. What is compassion? If you really had compassion in your life, what difference would it make to the way you live? What difference would it make to the policies of governments?
4. What responsibility does India have for feeding herself? What steps can Indians take to bring this about? (See the story about the Indian farmers in Resource Material.)
5. Why do you think the answer "does not always lie in doing it yourself"?
6. How do political rivalries and provincial selfishness affect the distribution of food? Give specific examples. Could ordinary people help to remedy this? If so, how?
7. What effect could "a new spirit of care, unselfishness and responsible co-operation" have on the feeding of the people of this country? Does this apply only to the nations of the West or does it apply to us? If so, in what ways?
8. What do you think is the most important sentence in this whole passage? Discuss the answers given.

DISCUSSION TOPICS

1. "There is enough in the world for everyone's need but not for everyone's greed. If everyone cared enough and everyone shared enough, everyone would have enough." Is this practical economics?
2. "Either I sacrifice my selfishness for my nation or my nation for my selfishness."

RESOURCE MATERIAL

A CUP OF RICE

Maisie Croft, a grandmother of seven, lives in Sheffield in the north of England. In December 1974 she heard on the radio a group of housewives discussing a "Housewives' Declaration". She was deeply impressed by part of it which said, "We will care about the standard of living and the true happiness of families across the world. Have we the right to get richer every year when so many are hungry?" About the same time she saw a television programme on the desperate plight of the starving families in Bangladesh and was very disturbed by it. One morning in a time of quiet she had the thought, "A cup of rice for Bangladesh from every household in the city and across the country."

"This thought persisted for three weeks," she said, "until I had to obey and do something about it. I discussed it with a friend and decided to go ahead." She told the Community Relations Officer for Sheffield, who came from Bangladesh, of her decision. He rang the High Commissioner who was very interested and asked to be kept informed. The local newspaper heard about this and published a photograph and a story. The radio interviewed her and this resulted in many letters from people wanting to collect rice.

"Next I obtained a certificate of exemption from the police for a door to door collection in my own district. I covered many streets taking a cup, a plastic bag and the "Housewives' Declaration". I have had very interesting conversations on my journeys round the streets and been uplifted at the response.

"The next concern was to find a room in the city centre where I could sit on a Friday, a busy shopping day, for people to bring their rice. I had the name of a church in the centre of the city and when I followed this up, the church officials gave me a room."

After four months and hundreds of visits, she had collected two tons of rice, which she and those she had enlisted packed into sixteen tea chests, six drums and six sacks, and had managed to get it shipped free by a Bangladesh shipping line. It was then distributed to the poor by the Bangladesh Girl Guides.

"WE WILL UPLIFT INDIA THROUGH HER SOIL"

Maruthi Yadav is a Maharashtrian farmer. In 1967 when this story begins, he was in his sixties and he had two brothers, Narayan Rao who was seventy and Kashav who was sixty and a former inspector of excise. They were now all farmers but for the last fifteen years there had been a "tug of war" between Maruthi and Narayan Rao as to who was more important.

One day, the three of them went to a meeting at a big new building which had been built on the hill top above their village. At the meeting the chairman said, "There are two voices in all of us, a good and a bad. Let us take time now to listen to the good and throw out the bad. Then we will express the thoughts we have had."

After the time of quiet those present were asked what thoughts they had had which they would like to contribute. Maruthi stood up. In front of Narayan Rao he read out what he had written down, "Ask your elder brother for his forgiveness for the years of bitterness and division."

"When will you do it?" asked the chairman.

"I'll do it here and now," he said and did.

Then Narayan Rao got up and said, "I am ready to forgive." After the meeting he turned to Maruthi. "What is this drama you created before other people?"

"It isn't a drama," said the younger brother. "I meant it."

In the months that followed the brothers tried to spread this spirit among the people and to apply it further in their own lives.

Narayan Rao, being old, was used to working two and a half hours a day to produce only what he needed. He had never fully cultivated his land. Soon he was using all of it, working six to seven hours a day. Production went up several times. He said, "India, too, must grow more than she needs for herself."

Narayan Rao died in 1970, but the two surviving brothers carried forward what he had begun. Maruthi has strong convictions about Indian agriculture. "We will uplift India through her soil," he once said. "Then we can have factories and other things added. But the key is the earth. We cannot compete with America in our factories but we can in our soil."

His farm has improved enormously, growing two crops in one year. It is more neatly kept, he enters the crops for local competitions and the village is now self-sufficient. He proudly says, "What I hoped to achieve in five years I have achieved in three through the unity we have found as brothers and in the spirit in the family."

TOPIC IX
3 to 4 lessons

The greatest power in the world

AIM

To study love as the motivating power for enduring constructive action.

DEVELOPMENT

What is the modern concept of love? What do films, pop songs, magazines etc. have to say about it?

Is there any difference between love, romance and sex? If so, what is it?

What do the different scriptures have to say about love? Let the class find this out for themselves, but the following are some suggestions:

Bhagavada Gita

The man who has good will for all, who is friendly and has compassion; who has no thought for "I" or "mine", whose peace is the same in pleasures and sorrows, and who is forgiving; ever full of joy, whose soul is in harmony and whose determination is strong: whose mind and inner vision are set on me — this man loves me and is dear to me.

Buddhist Scriptures

But if ill-will or the desire to hurt others should stir your mind, purify it again with its opposite, which will act on it like a wishing jewel on water. Friendliness and compassion are ... forever opposed to hatred as light to darkness.

Koran

Requite evil with good and he who is your enemy will become your dearest friend.

Bible

You shall love your neighbour as a man like yourself.

Love is patient; love is kind and envies no one. Love is never boastful, nor conceited nor rude, never selfish, not quick to take offence. Love keeps no score of wrongs; does not gloat over other men's sins, but delights in the truth. There is nothing that love cannot face; there is no limit to its faith, its hope and its endurance.

It is an interesting and challenging exercise to write out this last passage, but inserting one's own name in the place of the word "Love". Is this the sort of person you are?

What differences are there in these concepts of love from those you discussed at the beginning of the lesson?

Let the class each write down their own definition of absolute love. Then let each read out what he has written. Ask the class to give their views on what they feel are the most important points from what was read out.

Is love getting or giving?

What is more important for your happiness:

(a) giving love or (b) getting love?

Can people live really happy lives without love?

What happens to people who are not loved or do not love?

Mother Teresa has said, "The biggest disease today is not leprosy or tuberculosis, but rather the feeling of being unwanted, uncared for and deserted by everybody. The greatest evil is the lack of love and charity, the terrible indifference towards one's neighbour who lives at the roadside assaulted by exploitation, corruption, poverty and disease."

What effect can this lack of love and this terrible indifference have on the life of a nation?

You will do anything to please someone you love very much. Why? We sometimes find ourselves hurting those we love the most. Why is this? Are we meant to love our friends and the family whatever they do? Is it love to tolerate what is wrong? Someone said, "Hate the sin, but love the sinner". Discuss what this means.

If you really love people you will try to help them overcome the things in themselves which make them unhappy. To do this you may have to cross their wills and even make them angry.

GROUP DISCUSSION

1. "To be absolutely loving, an action must be honest, unselfish and pure in motive." What does the group think of this definition of love? Search together for examples from your own lives of actions you have seen or experienced which you consider were motivated by absolute love. What was the effect of these actions on the people concerned?

2. What is the connection between love and God? What makes people disbelieve in God? Is it sometimes because they see people who say they believe in God acting in an unloving way towards others? If those of us who believe in God really loved other people enough to put all our efforts into ending the injustices and wrongs in society, would it help those who do not believe, to find a faith? Why? How?

3. "You are as near to God as you are to the person from whom you feel most divided." Which is easier — to hate those who are unkind to you or who wrong you, or to love them? Is forgiving an enemy a sign of strength or weakness? (See Joseph's story in topic XII, page 113.)

ESSAYS

1. Do you believe that love is the greatest power in the world? Give your reasons and examples.

2. Find a true story to illustrate the power of love in a person's life and what he/she has been able to do because of it.

CONCLUSION

Have a time of prayerful silence when the students can think about the following, and write down any thoughts they get:

The test of your continuing maturity is your willingness to forgive those who offend you and to welcome always those whom you dislike.

Is there anyone in your life towards whom you should

start showing love rather than indifference or dislike?

Think through the situations in the world which could change if even one side started to live absolute love.

There should be a chance for the students to share with everyone the ideas they have had, if they so wish.

The power of silence

AIM

To discover the effective direction which can come from listening to the Inner Voice.

DEVELOPMENT

We live in an age of increasing noise — cars, jet planes, radios, electric guitars etc. Some people say that the present generation is afraid of silence. What do you think of this statement?

The following questions might help the students to think more about their attitudes to silence:

1. If you are alone do you choose a silent or creative activity or do you immediately put on the radio or T.V.?
2. If you are with a friend do you feel you have to talk all the time or can you be happy when there is silence between you?
3. What is your favourite kind of holiday? Does this involve a lot of noise and people or is it quiet?
4. Can you remember the last time you were somewhere where there was silence? Where was it and what did you feel?

Let the class sit silently for a few minutes and listen to the world around them. Let them make a list of the things they hear. How many of them were sounds which they had not noticed before? Do the students feel they have missed anything in life by not being aware of these sounds?

Some people are afraid of silence because of the things which may come to their mind. Let the class make another experiment of sitting quietly for a few minutes. This time ask them to write down the thoughts which come into their minds, however insignificant they may be. Some of the students may be willing to say what they have written down. Find out how many of them thought about problems or worries they have.

What do you do when you have a problem? Do you:

try and forget it?
talk about it and get other people's opinions?
keep it entirely to yourself and worry about it?
try reasoning out what the solution could be?

How effective are these methods in bringing a solution?

The following story is about a man who had a problem and how he found a solution:

Gajanan Sawant is a textile worker in a factory near Bombay. One day he went to an industrial seminar with a delegation from his mill. He went with a heart full of worries and problems. He was worried about the squalor in which his family and others were living in their chawl (village), but what could he, one man, do about it?

As he listened to the speakers at the seminar, he heard the experiences of many people who had discovered that unexpected solutions to problems can come from listening to the still, small voice inside every heart. Sawant decided to experiment with this idea. When he listened quietly to this Inner Voice, he had a simple but important thought. This was that he should start by cleaning up his village and clearing the well himself.

On his return home, he set to work picking up the rubbish between the houses and sweeping the mud paths clean. First the people watched and ridiculed him. Soon, however, the children fetched brooms and joined him. His next step was to buy a bucket and rope to clean the well. Here again his friends watched him as he lowered himself into the muddy, filthy well and started to clear it. One by one other men joined him until it became a village project. Eventually the well was cleared and clean water began to flow in.

There were other problems too. The children did not go to school as the municipal school is on the other side of an extremely busy highway, which is very hazardous to cross. So most of the children used to loiter around spending their time gambling and learning all sorts of other wrong things. One morning, during his time of silence Sawant had the thought, "Why not start a school here in my chawl?" He also had the thought to give up smoking and give the money he saved towards building the school. He told the villagers of this proposition and his decision to help finance it. They responded and soon they had collected enough money to build the school. They also found a teacher and raised the money to pay her a small salary.

In this way Sawant and his friends started a much needed social revolution in their village. As they began to experience a change of heart themselves, the Inner Voice of God led them step by step in dealing with the wrongs around them. They began to work for the good of everyone. The five men who own the village even responded. One of them said, "I was very impressed by the discipline and honesty with which you all worked. I would like to help you."

The results have been that many of the men have stopped gambling and drinking and their wives have more money for the food the families need. These men are also attending work regularly and so now have a steady income.

Because one man had the courage to start with himself and obey the thoughts given by the Inner Voice, seemingly insurmountable problems have been overcome and others are continuing to be tackled in the same spirit.

QUESTIONS

1. What was Sawant worrying about when he arrived at the seminar?
2. What experiment did he try there?
3. What ideas did he get?
4. What did he do when he returned to his village?
5. What result did this have on other people in the village?
6. How is it that the wives of the men have more money to spend on the things which are needed?
7. Do you have any problems which you would like to solve? What are they?
8. What does your Inner Voice tell you to do about them?

THE POWER OF SILENCE 97

Mahatma Gandhi said two interesting things about the Inner Voice:

"The Voice was more real to me than my own existence. It has never failed me, or for that matter, anyone else. And everyone who wills can hear the Voice."

"Like every other faculty, this faculty for listening to the still small voice within requires previous effort and training."

We have to have plenty of practice at listening to the still small voice. A musician or a sportsman or an actor has to have plenty of practice to become efficient in what he is doing. What happens to a piece of machinery which hasn't been used for a long time? What happens to the legs of someone who has had to spend a long time in bed?

Does the voice in our hearts always tell us the right thing?

Someone once said, "There are two voices which speak in every heart. Every day I have to take time to throw out the bad voice and listen to the good one."

Have you ever experienced hearing the good voice in your heart? When was this? Did you obey it? Why?

Why is it that we sometimes ignore the good voice in our hearts? Are there times when we don't even hear it? Why don't we hear it? Is it because it isn't always there or because there is something which stops us from hearing it? What can stop us hearing it?

The class should give their own suggestions in answer to these questions. Then, if it helps, the teacher can give the following illustration:

In a way, we are rather like a radio. If some dirt gets into a radio or a wire becomes detached, our radio goes dead or it makes buzzing noises so loudly that we can't hear what is being said. So, every time we do something wrong, and we do nothing to put it right, all our connections begin to get dirty and we stop hearing the voice of conscience. If we want to hear it again, we have to clean up our radio and get out all the dirt.

Some people call this voice, the voice of God. If He made the world, it is most likely that He has a plan for it.

Here are two other things Gandhiji said:

"The only tyrant in this world that I accept is the 'still, small voice' within."

"My firm belief is that He reveals himself daily to every

human being, but we shut our ears to the still, small voice."

Some of the class might like to find out more about what Gandhiji said on this and the part it played in his life.

In the Koran there is a saying, "An hour of listening is better than one thousand years of prayer."

A Chinese proverb says, "God gave men two ears and one mouth. Why don't we listen twice as much as we talk?"

It is important to help the students to see that the Inner Voice not only gives *correction*, but also *direction*. Each day can start with the question, "What does God want me to do?" and creative thoughts will often come. When obeyed, there may be most unexpected results.

God has a plan for everyone.

> God has a plan, you have a part,
> Oh every woman and man open your heart
> To the simple fact that God can guide you,
> By the voice you recognise deep inside you.
> For this is the voice that can bring the cure,
> Can heal the hurts and hates
> And peace secure.
> Oh every woman and man open your heart,
> God has a plan and you have a part.[1]

Let the class try again the experiment of sitting quietly and writing down their thoughts. Some may ask how they can know whether these ideas are their own or inspired by God. Not every thought comes from God, but we are more likely to hear that voice if we take time to listen than if we do not. Here also are three tests which can be applied:

1. Ask yourself, "Is this thought absolutely honest, absolutely pure, absolutely unselfish and absolutely loving?"
2. Share your thoughts with someone you can trust and who is also trying to do this experiment, to see what they think.
3. Carry out your ideas and see what happens. Obedience is an essential part of the experiment.

Note

It is suggested that the teacher should attempt this experiment himself before launching on it with the students. (Any personal experiences of the teacher will encourage the students to make a practice of listening.)

[1] A verse from the song on page 148.

This is an experiment well worth making and anyone can start. Gandhiji talked about listening *daily*. Why might this be a good idea? When do you think is a good time to do it?

It is also a good idea to write down the thoughts that you get. There is another Chinese proverb which says, "The strongest memory is weaker than the palest ink." If we write down each thought as it comes, our minds are then free to move on to the next thought. Also some of us can have very bad memories when we have uncomfortable thoughts!

Some of the class may like to try listening to their Inner Voice regularly every day. After some days, get them to report back to the class and tell of any changes there have been, e.g. situations or relationships which have changed; changes in their own attitudes on any points; answers found to problems etc.

ACTIVITIES

1. Essay topic: "A World of God's Design."
2. Some of the class could try to write a poem about their experiences of silence. Others could look for poems written by others about silence, stillness etc. Here are two verses written from an experience of quiet:

> Drop thy still dews of quietness
> Till all our strivings cease;
> Take from our souls the strain and stress,
> And let our ordered lives confess
> The beauty of thy peace.
>
> Breathe through the heats of our desire
> Thy coolness and thy balm,
> Let sense be dumb, let flesh retire;
> Breathe through the earthquake, wind and fire
> O still small voice of calm!
>
> —JOHN GREENLEAF WHITTIER.

Note for the Teacher
More stories can be found in other topics for further illustration of this concept of listening to the Inner Voice.

Once the students have learnt this habit, it can often be the solution for problems which arise in the classroom and the school. Once the student has got an idea from the Inner Voice, he is far more likely to carry it out than being told what to do by the teacher. Also the Inner Voice may demand far more of the students than the teacher would dare to demand. The following is a story of how one difficult problem was solved in this manner. It is told by the teacher:

"I was walking home on my return from a school outing to the theatre when a girl from my class greeted me. She got off her bicycle and started walking beside me. Very soon she was telling me that, while I had been out, they had been in trouble with another member of the staff. Evidently they had made her very angry, hot words had been exchanged and the class had been kept in after school. Dorothy filled in all the painful details carefully avoiding any mention of what the teacher had done.

"Next morning I was accosted by the teacher, as I entered the staff room. She was still extremely angry. She was rather surprised when I said that I knew what had taken place. She was even more surprised that I had not been told what she had said or done. However, she wanted me to go and give my class a thorough scolding for their extremely bad behaviour.

"I went to my classroom pondering what I should say or do. As I entered, a deathly hush fell on the class. Dorothy had told them that I knew all about it. Thirty-six pairs of eyes followed me to my desk. All the time the question was buzzing in my mind, 'What shall I say?' As I really did not know what to do, I stood and asked God to tell me. In the quiet of that moment, a clear thought came to me. 'Simply tell them to use the assembly time to think over what happened and what, if anything, they should do about it.'

"Every morning the school assembled for a time of worship together before classes began. So the class knew what I meant when I told them my thought.

"On returning after the assembly, one girl asked to go out. I did not question her, but allowed her to do so. Another student put her hand up and said, 'The teacher was wrong to call me the name she did, but I was more wrong for answering back. At break time I will go and say I am sorry.'

"Several months later, this same member of staff asked me, 'What exactly did you say to your class the day after they behaved so badly with me?' I told her. She then went on to say that often before, whole classes or groups representing classes had come and apologised to her, but this had been different. Every student had offered an apology individually over the next few days and they had been a very different class to teach ever since.

"These students had learnt a very precious lesson. If they wanted to do what was right then there was a voice in their hearts which would tell them what that was. They had taken action on that occasion, out of their own conviction and not because the teacher had told them to. In fact, the teacher had been ignorant of what they had done until she was told several months later."

People with a purpose

AIMS

To help the students to understand that the sort of people they are speaks more loudly than big words and that to be effective in life we must have a big enough purpose. This attitude is demonstrated by the story of a pupil who put up his hand, in the middle of his teacher giving them a bit of a lecture, and said, "Please sir, what you *are* is shouting so loudly that I can't hear what you *say*."

DEVELOPMENT

It is people with a purpose who have made history.

Ask the students to write down the names of five people whom they believe to have had a purpose in their lives. These people can either have lived in the past or still be alive. They can have affected the world for better or for worse. For example: Mao, Hitler, Lincoln, Gandhi, Mother Teresa, Wilberforce etc.

Write a list on the board, getting one name from each person in the class, if possible. Pick out about six of the names and ask the class these questions about them:

1. What was/is his/her aim in life? (Make sure they do not tell you merely what the person did. You want to find the underlying aim of each person. The story of William Wilberforce at the end of this topic will help to illustrate this.)
2. Which were those who had unselfish aims?

3. Which were those who had selfish aims?
4. What are the forces which can drive men and women on to do great things either good or bad — the forces which keep them going even when things are difficult?

Now ask the class to write down the name of someone they know personally whom they think has an aim in life. Do not ask them the name of this person, but ask:

1. What is his/her aim in life?
2. How do you know this? (It is usually through the kind of person they are, the things they do and how they do them.)

In the light of all that we have discovered about other people, ask the class:

1. On what do you spend your money?
2. How do you spend most of your spare time?
3. For whom do you use your creative talents?

Give them plenty of opportunity to express themselves on this. Then tell them that the way we spend our money, our spare time and creative talents is an indication of our aim in life.

Ask them to write down, for their own knowledge only, their own aims in life. Give them plenty of time to think this through. Then ask them to ask themselves the following questions:

1. Does this purpose benefit others?
2. Does it use all my creative abilities?
3. Will it be worth sacrificing for if this becomes necessary?
4. Is it such a big aim that I need others to help me fulfil it?
5. Will it help to bring about the changes I want to see in society?

Have a time of silence when they can ponder their answers. If they have answered "No" to most of the questions they may need to make some decisions in order to find a new purpose in life. If they have answered "Yes" to most of them they may need to consider whether they have the courage to stick to their purpose and also whether it needs to be made more effective. They may like to share their ideas with the class or they may have questions to ask and discuss with each other in order to clarify their ideas. It could be a help to divide them into small groups and let them spend some time on this topic.

When they have reached some conclusions, it would be worth their considering how their decision is going to affect the use of their money, spare time and creative abilities in practical terms. If they share with the rest of the class any decisions they have made on these things, then their friends can help them to keep them.

RESOURCE MATERIAL
WILLIAM WILBERFORCE

William Wilberforce was born in England in the year 1759. In those days much of Britain's wealth lay in the slave trade. British ships carried slaves from the coastal ports of West Africa to the West Indies. There they were sold in exchange for sugar. This sugar was then transported in the same ships to England where it was used to make rum as well as for domestic use. The British people hardly ever saw a slave in their own country and yet their men were running the slave ships. Very large sums of money were involved, thus affecting the British economy.

Four years before the birth of Wilberforce, the captain of a slave ship, Captain John Newton, had an experience which changed his life. One day he discovered that his sailors had been throwing overboard slaves who were dying but were still alive. This horrified him. On questioning the sailors, he found that often, when a slave became very ill and near death, he would be thrown overboard, to make more room for the others and to prevent the disease from spreading. This inhumanity struck deeply into the heart of John Newton. When he arrived back into an English port once more, he left his ship, never to return. With this experience still engraved in his heart, he began to search for ways to end this terrible wrong.

Some years later he met William Wilberforce, who at twenty-one had become the youngest member of the British parliament. Wilberforce was a brilliant orator, and the closest friend of the Prime Minister, William Pitt. This meant that any position of power was available to him. However, through meeting Newton, and understanding his passion to abolish the slave trade, Wilberforce decided to take this on as his priority in life.

For ten years he battled away. Each year he introduced a bill in Parliament to abolish the slave trade and each year it was defeated. He knew that in every year that passed, he had failed to save the lives of 50,000 black men, women and children. Then, after ten years, he was given the promise that his bill would be passed — on condition that he supported the continued appointment of a colleague, whom he knew to be corrupt. He refused.

For the next ten years he kept fighting to awaken the conscience of his colleagues and of the nation. He enlisted everyone he could and finally in 1807 the bill abolishing the slave trade by British ships was passed.

Here was a young man who could have had wealth, power and position. He deliberately turned it down in order to fight what he considered to be a deep moral wrong in his nation.

"He risked his reputation, sacrificed his career, brought on himself the dislike of the King, the anger of the Establishment and the fierce opposition of politicians, church leaders and businessmen. He endangered his life, impaired his health and spent his fortune. And he lived to see his work accomplished, whereby humanity took one of its boldest and best steps forward in the whole of history."[1]

This was one battle which Wilberforce took on and a big one. However, he also felt called to change many other wrong attitudes in the country, in people both high and low. He created a whole new climate in British political life and pioneered political integrity in an age of corruption. His fight laid the foundation for the many social reforms which took place in the following years such as the outlawing of the employment of women and children in the coal mines.

More details about William Wilberforce and other examples of "People with a Purpose" can be found in *Brave Men Choose* by Garth Lean (Blandford Press, London).

---

[1] From the preface to the play *Mr Wilberforce M.P.* by Alan Thornhill (Blandford Press). We recommend this play as a playreading in your class, followed by a full discussion.

Turning enemies into friends

AIMS

To learn how to turn enemies into friends starting with our personal relationships with others. To see that this art of healing and reconciliation is the one most needed in the world today and one which we can all learn.

DEVELOPMENT

Questionnaire: let the students write down the answers to the following questions so that they can be discussed later:

1. Write down the things which make you lose your temper.
2. What do you do when you lose your temper?
3. Do you ever feel like hitting out and throwing things?
4. Does this make the situation better or worse?
5. What does this do a) to you, and b) to the other person?
6. Do you think these feelings of yours could have anything to do with the violence we see around the world today?
7. What are the things which make you angry and bitter?
8. Do you blame other people for these? If so, why?
9. You may not hate anyone, but is there anyone whom you do not like or anyone you just ignore? Why?
10. If you hate or even dislike someone can you help him/her to change?
11. It is the people we do not like whom we think need to change the most. Can you suggest any way in which you could start to bring a change in a situation like this?

When the class has had enough time to answer these questions, take each question in turn and see what experiences and opinions there are on each. Discuss the issues raised. You may find that one particular question catches their imagination and is worth taking in more detail. The class could then be split into small groups so that more of them get a chance to express their views and share their experiences.

The following material may help during the class discussions on questions 6 to 11 above.

Question No. 6
(a) Why do people turn to violence?
(b) Are the results they want really achieved through violence?
(c) Does one have to destroy completely the old before one can build a new society?
(d) Can a society achieved through violence be maintained without violence?

Questions No. 7 and 8
We need to hate what is wrong in the world — injustice, oppression, exploitation. We need to deal with them in society, but they have their roots in the human heart. That is where they first need to be tackled.
(a) For instance, is there any injustice, oppression or exploitation in your homes and school?
(b) Injustice — am I ever unjust to others?
(c) Oppression — do I ever impose my will on others and insist on them doing what I want them to do?
(d) Exploitation — do I ever expect people to do things which I am not prepared to do myself? Do I ever expect people to do things for me — to serve me — when I am not prepared to serve them? In fact, do I *use* people?

Note
The teacher will find it quite easy to learn from the students where they feel these things are used against them by others, but it is far more important that they recognise when they do it to others because that is a place where they can start to put it right.

Question No. 9
Indifference is as bad as hate, because we just don't care at all about these people. Indifference and dislike of people stem

from the same root in our heart as hate. A famous black American educator said, "Nobody shall drag me down so low as to make me hate him."

What does hate do to people? Does it affect the person who is hating? (The class will have suggestions on this.) Here are some additional points that come from those who have experienced hate in their hearts.

(a) It lowers a person in his own eyes.
(b) It blinds him to reality and colours his thinking.
(c) It makes the person its slave because it completely determines his actions.
(d) It often brings out the worst in people.
(e) It can make them mentally unbalanced and affect their physical health.
(f) If one hates anyone, one cannot then truly care for other people however hard one tries.
(g) Sometimes hate causes people to hurt the very people they love. (Hate releases a poison into one's heart and this often breaks out in temper or impatience with those whom you love.)
(h) A person who feels wronged can often become full of self-pity. This self-absorption will gradually cut out other people and turn to bitterness inside.
(i) It makes one believe that the person against whom one feels hatred is always wrong in everything he says and does. It equally makes oneself feel always right. This is a lie because no one person can *always* be right nor *always* wrong.

Conrad Hunte, the former Vice-Captain of the West Indies cricket team said, "Those who have suffered most have the most to give in the task of humanising society." (*Playing to Win*, Himmat Publications). Having found the cure to these feelings, they can be sure that the same wrongs and injustices are not experienced by others.

One important thing to remember is that our task is to "Hate the sin but love the sinner."

Questions No. 10 & 11
If someone you do not like comes along and tells you all the places where he/she thinks you are wrong, does this make you

want to be a better person? It does not. In fact it usually makes you angry and determined to stay the way you are. If however, someone we love and respect says where he/she thinks we should try to be different and perhaps also tells of an instance from his/her own experience of having to change a wrong attitude, we usually consider it seriously and try our best to improve. If this is true of ourselves and the way we react, we may need to examine the way we treat others, in this light.

QUOTATIONS

Oh you don't love God if you don't love your neighbour,
If you gossip about him, if you never have mercy,
If he gets into trouble and you don't try to help him.
Then you don't love your neighbour and you don't love God.[1]

Please, thank you and sorry, simple to say it's true,
Not so simple or easy when you really mean it too.
An unfailing manoeuvre for bringing a fight to an end,
And a practical tip if you're wanting to turn an enemy into a friend.

— from the film, *Give a Dog a Bone*[2]

"If you are only 1% wrong and the other person is 99% wrong, it is much easier for you to apologise for your 1% than he for his 99%."

ACTIVITY

Let the class write plays or stories, illustrating some of the points expressed in the discussion on the above quotations.

The Koran says: "Requite evil with good and he who is your enemy will become your dearest friend."
Tao-ist scripture says: "Return love for great hatred."
Pocket World Bible: "Hatred does not cease by hatred at any time: hatred ceases by love — this is an old rule."
The Bible says: "I say love your enemies! Pray for those who persecute you. ... If you love only those who love you, what good is that? Even scoundrels do that much."

[1] A verse from the song, on page 152.
[2] A verse from the song, on page 150.

Through the different scriptures God has told man that he must answer hate with love. He would not have told us to do that if He did not have the power to replace love in our hearts where we have harboured hate. If we want to overcome hate in our hearts, there are two things we can do: first, we can decide to start treating the people we have hated differently and put right anything that has been wrong on our side. Secondly we can pray to God that he will help us love these people and ask Him to remove the hate from our hearts. It has been experienced by many that when one does this a feeling of peace comes into one's heart and it seems to help one see the other person in such a different way that it appears that they have changed too!

DISCUSSION QUESTIONS

1. Does it take more courage to love people enough to change them than to hate them? If so, why?
2. Is it true love to tolerate in a person or a country things which are wrong? Are there wrong things which you have tolerated a) in your family b) in the school c) in the community? What can you do about them?
3. A man who has suffered greatly said, "I realise that I have been too sensitive to how much *others* have hurt me and have forgotten how much I have hurt others." In what ways could a change of heart like this affect the situation in the world today?

STORIES WITH QUESTIONS

The following are two true stories of young men. One shows how a young person found a better way than violence to put right the wrongs he saw in society. The other illustrates that there is a stronger power than hate which can change an enemy into a friend.

Kishore comes from Jamshedpur. This is in Bihar and is the home of the Tata Iron and Steel Company. It was built by the Tata family as a "model" town for their workers. It has many amenities which other Indian towns do not have. Yet it has been the centre of a great deal of violence in past years.

When Kishore was still at school, he used to see his father going to work every morning wearing a clean shirt and returning in the evening exhausted and with his shirt covered with grease from the work he had done in the factory. He also saw other men, who had office jobs, returning home from work looking as clean and fresh as when they had left in the morning. He began to ask himself why there should be this difference.

Kishore's eldest brother was, at this time, a militant revolutionary and Kishore admired his courage and passion. He joined him in his bid to end exploitation and free the working class. From the age of thirteen he was trained in the use of violence. He and his friends often went and lived in the villages with the poorest people and organised them in their revolution of hate. They caused terror at school and tears and despair at home. Kishore was hardly fifteen when he was first arrested.

One day in his school he heard someone speak of how human nature can be changed. The speaker gave examples of this change in the hearts of men across the world. Kishore was interested. The fact that to change society you should start by changing yourself appealed to his logical mind. But he had learnt to trust no one. So he and his friends went often to the hostel where Ravindra Rao, the man who had spoken, was staying. They asked many questions and watched everything. Anything nice in the room they would examine and then put down muttering, "Capitalist!" One day Ravindra said to them, "If I have something you don't then I become a capitalist, don't I?" Unexpectedly Kishore stopped and then said, "Come to think of it, that has been my attitude all along. At that rate there is no end to it. Even I may be regarded as a capitalist by some."

Some time later Ravindra Rao invited them to come to a camp. He said, "See how this idea works. If you find it is better, accept it!" They went. On the way they had breakfast at a cafe. After paying the bill and leaving, Ravindra discovered that he had been undercharged. He went back and paid the difference. Kishore and his friends said to him later, "After that we didn't need to go to the camp. We knew you must be genuine."

At the camp they could hardly believe what they saw — black, white, brown, Europeans, Africans, Asians, Brahmins and Harijans, bosses and workers, all working together. The care shown to them melted their hate. "This," they thought, "is the real revolution." They decided to be a part of it.

They put right the things which they had done wrong. Many apologies were made to the school principal, teachers, parents and friends whom they had cheated or assaulted. Some returned money to the State Transport for travelling ticketless on the buses. Many of their friends changed and their number grew.

"To be 'good' was not our goal. 'Jamshedpur should be a model city', was the thought from the inner voice. We set out to tackle the wrongs around us."

They wrote a play to tell others of what they had found. It was seen by over 3,000 people. When an unofficial strike broke out in the city, they met union leaders. Afterwards they were told that their efforts had helped towards a settlement.

Kishore and his friends feel fully responsible for changing their country. "It is not difficult to get people to do what you want at a bayonet point," says one of them. "But it is temporary. Change of heart is permanent."

QUESTIONS

1. What was it that made Kishore bitter and violent?
2. What convinced Kishore and his friends that Ravindra Rao was living what he talked about?
3. How did Kishore and his friends begin to make amends for what they had done in the past?
4. Are there apologies that you need to make for your bad temper?
5. Are there situations which you need to put right, which have been caused by your trying to force other people to do what you wanted?
6. Do you have the sort of love and care for other people which overcomes their hate and bitterness?
7. Are there some people whom you simply dislike, but for whom you need to find a new attitude?
8. How and when will you deal with these things in your life so that you can help others to do the same?

Joseph comes from Mizoram in the North-East of India. But for nearly ten years he lived in Bhutan, Tibet and Sikkim, where his father worked with the Indian Mission. In 1964 his father retired and put all his savings into setting up radio agencies and a cinema hall, the only one in that part of the Mizo Hills.

A year later came the beginning of the armed uprising in the Mizo Hills. Their home, their shop and the cinema hall were totally destroyed. With all their income gone, the family had to run away elsewhere. Joseph's father was imprisoned. Joseph was then eighteen. "An intense bitterness and hate gripped my heart," he says. "I made up my mind to do my worst when the time came. But for the time being I had to earn my living and get some education."

He joined night school in Shillong and earned his way cooking and washing dishes, doing odd jobs on construction sites and polishing the shoes of government officers early in the morning. But the earnings were too uncertain to support himself and his family. So he turned to music and formed a pop group which became known throughout the area. Their broadcasts on All India Radio brought fan mail even from Burma and Pakistan.

By March 1970 he had decided that he would join his guerilla friends fighting in the jungle. But at this point his love of music took him to see a show which had come from Europe, and which was being performed in Shillong. He was fascinated by the music, but above all he was gripped by the answer to hate which he saw portrayed in some of the scenes.

"I was deeply challenged," he said, "that if I wanted to build a new society and see the world free from hate, poverty and injustice, the best place to start was with myself. I did not believe that my burning hate could change, but I decided to try. I attempted to listen to God, but I did not get any extraordinary thoughts except a feeling to be honest with my father and to put things right in my life."

This meant apologising to his brothers and sisters for the way he had treated them. He also gave up drugs. He had been smoking hashish for a year. "I saw my friends doing it. I was frustrated and bitter. I will die soon anyway, I thought, so why not try?" He also wrote to various people asking their forgiveness for his hatred.

A month later he was at a conference in the west of India.
An Indian army officer was there. Joseph says, "The thought
which challenged me the most was to forgive the people whom
I had blamed for the suffering of my family, particularly that
of my father. It took me a week to decide to ask God for help."
Finally he sought out this army officer and told him the story
of his life, of his desire for revenge and how he was now
seeking a new solution. "Please forgive me for my hatred of
men like you," he said. The officer was shaken and said to
Joseph, "Thank you very much for what you have said. The
change in you is not the work of an ordinary man."

Joseph said later, "That moved me very much and I
began to see that if I spoke honestly from my heart, even my
opponents would understand. Where I could not change them
through the barrel of a gun, I succeeded with a change of
heart."

QUESTIONS

1. In this story Joseph apologised to the people who he felt
   had been responsible for his family's suffering. Why did
   he do this?
2. Is it essential for people to forgive their enemies if they
   are to turn them into friends? Give your reasons.
3. Are there people to whom you need to apologise? Could
   you do it before next lesson in order to give other people
   the courage to follow your example?

ACTIVITIES

1. It may be possible to develop some of the plays written
   earlier so that they can be used with other classes in the
   school to express what they have been learning or ex-
   periencing in "Turning Enemies into Friends".
2. Some students may like to write a story of personal experiences like Kishore's and Joseph's, which could be used
   in the school paper or magazine.

Standing alone

AIMS

To find out how to conquer fear and find the source of courage.

DEVELOPMENT

There is a poem which reads:
> Dare to be a Daniel,
> Dare to stand alone,
> Dare to have a purpose true,
> Dare to make it known.

Find out from the class if they know who Daniel was, what he did and what his purpose was.

The following is the story:

Daniel was a young man who lived in Jerusalem in the 6th century BC. In 586 BC Jerusalem was attacked and defeated by the Babylonians and Daniel was taken off as a prisoner. However, as he was a fine strong and intelligent young man, it was decided that he should be brought up with the Babylonian princes. These men were given a daily allowance of food from the King's table. Daniel was afraid that this rich food would take his thoughts away from God, whom he had been brought up to put first in his life. So he asked if he could have plainer food. The man in charge of them was afraid to do this, in case Daniel became thin and ill. The King would then be cross. However, Daniel finally persuaded him and he found that Daniel did well on this food.

Some time later the King had a dream. He called in all his advisors and wise men to explain it to him. They tried to make all sorts of excuses but it was clear that they didn't know what it meant. The King lost his temper and ordered them all to be killed. Daniel was included in this order, but he courageously asked the King to give him time to think about the meaning of the dream. That night he prayed to God and God told him the meaning of the dream. The next morning he told the King, who was delighted and made him a governor over a whole province of Babylon.

Daniel was also advisor to the next kings. He became so popular and powerful that some people were jealous of him. They tried to think how to get rid of him. Yet he was so honest and efficient that they could not find anything to criticise. So they thought up a trick which would force the King to punish Daniel. Some of the princes went to the King and suggested that he should give an order that for thirty days nobody should pray to any other man or God than the King. If anyone did so, he should be thrown into the lions' den.

The King must have been rather a vain man, because unfortunately he agreed to do this. When he had approved the order, the princes said to him, "Remember the laws of this land that once the King's order has been given, it can never be altered." The King said that he would remember.

Daniel was in the habit of praying three times a day. Although he knew of the King's decree he continued to do so — not quietly in a corner where nobody would see, but he knelt in front of his open windows. The princes watched him do this and then quickly went away to the King to tell him. The King saw how he had been tricked and tried in every way that he could to save Daniel. The princes would not relent and finally he had to give in. Sadly he gave the order for Daniel to be thrown into the lions' pit. Before the pit was sealed, he said to Daniel, "Your own God whom you serve continuously will save you." Then a stone was rolled across the mouth of the pit and the king sealed it.

The King ate nothing and could not sleep the whole night. At dawn he hurried in fear and trembling to the pit and called out to Daniel. When he heard Daniel reply he was overjoyed. On being lifted out of the pit, no trace of injury was found on Daniel, because he had put his faith in God and God had protected him. After this no one tried to hurt Daniel again and he lived in the palace until he died a very old man.[1]

QUESTIONS

Let the students write down the answers.

1. What were the occasions on which Daniel had to make difficult decisions?
2. Did he have anyone who backed him up and stood with him?
3. How did he find the courage to make these decisions?
4. What is the difference between physical courage and moral courage? Which is harder, if either, and why?
5. What sort of things require moral courage? If you can, give examples from your own experience and knowledge.
6. Sometimes seemingly small things require a great deal of courage. Describe an occasion on which you did something which you found very difficult. How did you find the courage to do it?

Use the answers to these questions as a basis for discussion.

Does having courage mean that you are never afraid? It means doing what needs to be done, however we may feel. One man, when asked what he found was the answer to fear replied, "I think what I would do if I wasn't afraid and then I go and do it." Courage is God-given. When we step out and do what we know we should, then we find that God gives us the courage to carry it through. We have to make the start. If we don't take the first step, then we won't find the courage.

Get the class to write down all the things they are afraid of and the reasons why.

Some of our fears are imaginary. We imagine what *might* happen to us, but we don't *know* that it will. Are any of your fears like that? We are afraid of the unknown. Sometimes it helps to tell your fears to a good friend. They sometimes look very silly when you do this!

Next time you are afraid, make the experiment of going ahead as if you were not afraid and see what happens. By facing our fears, they lose their hold on us. At the next lesson some of the class may wish to tell of their experiences in doing this.

1 Adapted from *God's Hand in History* by Mary Wilson.

ESSAY

Write out the story of someone who had courage, including if you can, the source of this courage.

RESOURCE MATERIAL

The following is a story which may also be used, of a lady of our times who showed both moral and physical courage.

Mrs van Beuningen was a Dutch lady and this story took place during the last world war. The Germans had invaded her country and a concentration camp was built very near her home. Thousands of men, women and children were imprisoned there. The conditions in the camp were very bad. There was much illness, no medical supplies and people were dying of hunger. Mrs van Beuningen could not sleep for thinking of these people. One morning she decided to ask God what to do about this situation. She had previously spoken to a friend who had suggested she saw the Camp Commandant, but her husband was quite against it. That morning the thought came, "Have no fear. Don't treat him as an enemy, and try and reach his heart." So off she went.

The Commandant was so surprised that a Dutch lady should dare walk into the camp, that he agreed to see her. They talked together for two hours. Finally she found that his soft spot was his love for his son, who was fighting in Russia. This was her clue, so she said, "Your son might land in a concentration camp too and what would you think if someone were to send him an extra package of food?"

"Naturally I would be very glad," he replied.

"Well," said Mrs van Beuningen, "I feel absolutely sure that if you give me permission to send in food to my countrymen, your son will be helped in Russia." The Commandant argued, but finally she got the permission to send in the food.

Although food was very severely rationed and the people were very short themselves, Mrs van Beuningen got all her friends and neighbours to eat a little less and to save every scrap of food. Within ten days the news of what she was doing had spread all over the country and people came from all over the place with every bit of food they could spare.

All went well for a few months, then suddenly the Com-

mandant was dismissed. A second man came and the food
parcels were returned. So she went to the camp again and
finally talked him over. Then a third man came who not only
sent back the parcels but who was absolutely determined not
to see her. This state of affairs lasted for ten days. Mrs van
Beuningen again asked God what she should do. She then had
the thought to keep on and on at the Commandant. Every day
she sent a letter, made a telephone call and sent a message by
people to ask him why he would not see her. At last he was
so angry that he agreed, but he said that he wanted to see
her in her own house, thinking that she would not do that.

Mrs van Beuningen did not know what to do. She knew
that many Dutch people would not like it if she received such
a man in her home. So she again asked for guidance. The
thought she had was, "Does the good opinion of people mean
more to you than the lives of those prisoners?" So she allowed
him to come. Her husband protested and left the house. On
the appointed day the Commandant arrived with six officers,
in full ceremonial dress. She thought, "They are coming to
take me." But immediately it was as if a voice spoke to her,
"Have no fear. It is the Commandant who matters."

For three hours they talked and she could get nothing
out of him but, "No, no, no!" She was absolutely at a loss to
know what to do. Suddenly the thought came, "Tell him he
has a kind heart." She thought to herself, "That man a kind
heart? Impossible!" But the thought kept on coming. Finally
she said, "Well now, we have been fighting for the whole
afternoon and you keep on saying, 'No, no, no'. But I know
that you have a good heart and deep in your heart you want to
give me the permission." The officers were trying very hard
not to laugh at the idea of the Commandant having a good
heart. He was very nervous and fidgeted in his chair. Finally
he burst out laughing and said, "All right, you have won."

He kept his word until very near the end of the war. One
day, when the liberation of the country was very near, Mrs van
Beuningen got a scribbled note from one of the prisoners saying
that they had heard that 500 of them were going to be shot
and the rest were to be taken away to Germany as hostages.
"You are the only person we can think of who can help us,"
the note continued. She had already been warned that the
camp commandant had placed soldiers with machine guns at

the approaches to the camp with orders to shoot at sight everyone who had no official reason for coming to the camp.

It was a difficult position, but Mrs van Beuningen realised
that it was her life or those of the prisoners. She again asked
God for guidance and the thought came, "Have no fear. Go
and see the Commandant." She went through the woods and
immediately saw a group of soldiers pointing their machine
guns at her and calling her to halt. She called back that she
wanted to speak to them and continued calmly walking towards
them. They were so astonished that they let her go on and
this happened with group after group until she reached the
last sentry. He agreed to telephone the Commandant and she
heard the Commandant yelling back that he had no time to
see her. She took hold of the telephone and told him what
she had heard about the plan to shoot 500 prisoners and that
it would be a terrible thing to do and that he would be heavily
punished for it. He gave her his word that none would be
executed. Then she asked about the hostages who were going
to be sent to Germany. "Well," he said, "what do you want
me to do?"

"Let them go free," said Mrs van Beuningen, "and I will
come and fetch them and see that they go home safely."

"Very well," he said at last. "You can come and fetch the
women and children tomorrow."

The next day she gathered together all the friends who
had some kind of vehicle and every available Red Cross car
and got the women and children away. The day after that
the Commandant 'phoned her and told her that she could
take the rest of the hostages.[1]

[1] Adapted from *A New World for My Grandchildren* by Charlotte
van Beuningen, Himmat Publications.

Homes—the backbone of a nation

AIMS

To help the students to understand the importance of united homes in the life of the nation. To find out how to create the spirit of a real home.

DEVELOPMENT

What is a family tree?

Can you draw a family tree of your immediate family?

The teacher may need to draw an example of a simple family tree, such as the one shown below. However, get the students to put in the names of people and not just the relationships as shown here. You may find that some students want to do a more complicated one depending upon how much they know or can find out about their families.

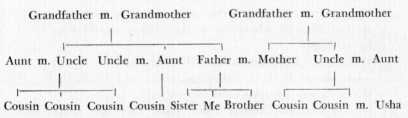

Grandfather m. Grandmother　　Grandfather m. Grandmother

Aunt m. Uncle　Uncle m. Aunt　Father m. Mother　Uncle m. Aunt

Cousin Cousin Cousin Cousin Sister Me Brother Cousin Cousin m. Usha

Put a coloured ring around those who live in the same house or compound as you.

Why do you think we live in families?

Let the students give their ideas first but the following are some suggestions:

1. Protection and care when the children are young.
2. Education — what sort of things are taught in the home?
3. Love and affection.
4. Companionship with parents and children and between parents.
5. Care of the old.

DEBATE

"The traditional (Indian) joint family is the best system."
Have speakers who will speak for and against this proposition and then take a vote in the class.
What is the difference between a house and home?
Note:
House — a building in which you live.
Home — the atmosphere created by those living in the house.
What makes an ideal home?

Write down your answers to the following questions. Give the students enough time to think about what they write.

1. Do you think your home should be a place where you can do just what you want all the time? Should you show consideration for others sometimes? Give examples.
2. What is your home like first thing in the morning? Is there peace and quiet or rush and hurry and sometimes frayed tempers?
3. Are you bright and cheerful early in the morning?
4. Does what happens in the home in the morning affect the way you feel and behave for the rest of the day at school?
5. Do you think this is the same for your father at work? If your father leaves home angry what is he likely to do at the office or where he works? What would happen if he is happy?
6. What are the arguments usually about in your home? Who starts them? Is there something you could do about these? Write down any practical suggestions.
7. If everyone was honest about what they felt would that make a difference in the home?
8. Do your parents and older people criticise you — your clothes, how you use your leisure etc? Are they right in some of their criticisms?
9. How important are material possessions in making a

happy home? Give your reasons.

10. What is your part in making your home an enjoyable place in which to live?

Use the students' answers to these questions as a basis of a practical discussion on how each one can help to bring the right spirit into his or her home.

The following story is how one girl managed to do this:

Ruth was thirteen and had twin brothers aged four and both her parents went out to work. She had to get up early in the morning to dress her two brothers, make their breakfast and then take them to school before she went herself. She never had any breakfast. She was very unhappy about this situation and what made matters worse, she was very worried about her mother who still went to work, although the doctor said that she was risking her health.

One day a friend suggested to Ruth that they should be quiet for a while and see what to do about all this. They were standing in the school corridor at the time, but they just stopped talking and were quiet for a few minutes. Then Ruth said, "I know what I should do. I should go home straight after school every day, clean the home and prepare the evening meal for the family. I shouldn't go rushing off with my friends, but really care for our home."

This was a difficult decision, but she knew in her heart that it was the right thing to do. So, even after a few weeks, when everything seemed still to be the same, she stuck to it. Some of her friends even started helping! One day, quite a long time afterwards, Ruth came to school looking very happy. She said, "My mother has decided to leave her job and look after the house and all of us. Dad comes home every evening instead of going out drinking with his friends and we are all much happier."

1. What was it that made Ruth's mother give up her job?
2. Why did her father start coming home and stop drinking?
3. What made Ruth stick to her decision?

How do the ideas and attitudes which we take from our homes affect the nation?[1]

---

[1] See the story under Resource Material (page 124) to illustrate this.

How could your home become a place where everyone who comes to it can see:
1. That families can be fun?
2. That homes can be places where adults and children enjoy each other's company?
3. That they are places where problems can be solved?

DISCUSSION TOPICS

1. "A family of united nations is made up of nations of united families."
2. There is no generation gap — only an honesty gap.

ACTIVITIES

Let the students write some short plays or stories on the things which they have learnt through this topic, using their own experiences as far as possible.

Suggest the class tries using the words "Please", "Thank you" and "Sorry" as often as they can at home, and see if there are any practical results. Has it affected their attitudes towards the people in their home? Towards their younger brothers and sisters? Towards the servants? How?

RESOURCE MATERIAL

The following story is an example of how change in the family can have far-reaching effects.

Robert Carmichael was a French jute manufacturer. He was known as a tough employer, respected by other employers, but feared by his men. He ruled his family as he ruled his workers. Argument was no good. He always knew what was best.

One day an unexpected phone call came to his home. A young man spoke on the other end of the line. He said he was an Englishman, Captain John Caulfeild. Could he please come to lunch?

Who was this fellow and what did he want? The family was curious. They told him he was welcome.

The Second World War had just ended. Over lunch they discussed the sad state of Europe. In France family life was badly upset. They all agreed that this must be put right if France was to become a strong nation again.

When the meal was over the young man made an unusual suggestion. Would they join him in a few moments of quiet to see what God had to say to them? Robert and his wife, although religious, were embarrassed. They had never done anything like that before and wondered what would happen. The two girls, their daughter and a niece, were enthusiastic. They produced paper and pencils to write down their thoughts and were immediately busy scribbling away.

After a time they were asked what they had written. The girls said that they wanted to be honest about their resentments against their parents. Two things in particular upset them. One was the way father ruled the family. The other was that they felt their parents did not live up to the beliefs they professed. The parents told the girls that they used the home like a hotel.

"Oh dear!" thought the young man as he left. "Have I stirred up a family row?"

If he had, it proved to be a healthy row. Resentments were now out in the open where they could be dealt with. Gradually the members of the family came to see where they had been wrong and the atmosphere started to change.

Carmichael decided to start each day by trying to find God's will. He had the pressing thought that he always put profit before people and that he had no larger aim than the success of his business. He decided to put his business life into God's hands.

Because he had decided to care for people, he was able to make friends with the Marxist secretary of the trade union. The trust which was built between them led to an historic agreement being reached in 1953 which affected the whole of the French textile industry. It meant immediate wage rises for 600,000 workers. These rises continued every year, production increased and the industry thrived. The spirit of this agreement lasted for over twenty years and led the revival of French industry.

Carmichael's thoughts were also going further afield. During a visit to Calcutta in 1951 he had the thought, "You are responsible for the millions in India and Pakistan who cultivate jute and who are dying of hunger." As he returned from India, he felt he must take this thought seriously. He decided to make sure that the employers in Europe paid a fair price for their jute and that this higher price must go to the workers in India and Pakistan.

He had set himself a difficult task. Most of the jute manufacturers did not want to pay higher prices. However Carmichael persisted and after two years he persuaded them to form the European Association of Jute Industries. He was the first president — a post he held for twelve years. However, his work to change people's attitudes continued. It was only in 1965, at a stormy session of the FAO in Rome that his aim was achieved. A new agreement was signed giving a fair fixed price for jute, higher wages to the growers and other necessary reforms. This was the first agreement for fixing the price of a commodity of which the Third World produced the largest part. It was followed by other such agreements.

This was a long way from the change which began with the young Englishman's visit. Yet without this initial start in the family, it is likely that none of these changes would have happened.

Using our gifts

AIMS

To help the students to find their place and task in the world and to make the most of the gifts they are given.

DEVELOPMENT

Show the class a number of diagrams with something missing, e.g. a flower with a petal missing, a face with an eye missing, a butterfly with a wing missing etc. Ask the class what they notice about all these pictures.

The design is not complete. So God's design for the world is not complete until everyone fulfils his part. To do this each person has been given particular gifts. What gifts like this can you think of? (Besides the more obvious ones, include the less obvious — making a home, a sense of humour, making friends etc.) Everyone has something which he is good at. Write down the talents which you think you have.

Whatever gifts a person has, God has put them there for a purpose. He means us to use them to the full. If they are not used, part of his design for the world is spoilt. Can you think of any reasons which would make people not want to use the gifts which God has given them?

Write a list of all the very talented people you can think of — either alive today or in the past. What would we not have in the world today if these people had not used their gifts?

We can use these gifts either for ourselves or for the good

of other people. In what ways can we use them selfishly? Why do we sometimes want to use them selfishly?

Do you think that talents can be developed?

Thomas Edison, the famous American inventor, said "Genius is one per cent inspiration and ninety-nine per cent perspiration." What do you think he meant by this?

Using your talents often involves a lot of hard work. This can be illustrated by the story of Sir Ronald Ross and of how he discovered which of the two thousand species of mosquitoes that exist was the carrier of the malaria parasite. (See under Resource Material, page 130.)

What do you think it was that made Ross go on and on as he did?

What other things do you think make people develop and use their talents to the full? What reasons would make you use your gifts to the full for the sake of other people?

The following is an article from a school magazine in Jamaica. Study it and then answer the questions at the end.

WHAT'S THE USE?

"What's the use of working?" somebody asked. "What's the use of going to school?" another asked. And yet another said, "What's the use of living?" These are questions people are asking today.

Many people don't see much in work these days. They define it as "that which is done in exchange for pay" usually between the hours of eight to five — and have long since shifted their attention to how to spend their leisure time.

With advances in science and technology, man has lost the pride and satisfaction he formerly had in his work. Technology has shifted the blame from him to the machine. He has lost the sense of achievement that he used to have and ends up asking himself, "What's the use?"

Gone are the days when a man could feel he was actually achieving something between eight and five. Gone are the days of the old grandmother who would get up at the crack of dawn to milk the cows, feed the hens and do a hundred other things. ... Her day's work was not a short spell from eight to five. She could work all day and still find delight in her work. Are those days gone? I suppose they have for the person who has lost the point of the job he is doing. ...

Perhaps the answer lies in looking at our situation again and deciding to try and do something useful with it. Whether you're a lowly worker, a barber, a storekeeper or whether you get milk from the cow or sell it in a store, this is no time for you to say, "What's the use?" ... Think! Think positively. It's no time to throw anything away. It's time to serve with all the strength that God gave you.

A patient was once asked why she left her home town to go to a distant hospital when there was a good one near her. "Yes," she replied, "but the hands were different". ... I guess that's what we want in our work, our school, in everything — special hands that are ready to serve with all the strength given to them by the Supreme Being.

Answer the following questions:

1. What sort of work gives you a sense of achievement?
2. If you do your best, are you more satisfied than if you try to get away with the least amount of work possible? Why?
3. In what ways have the advances of science and technology taken away the pride and satisfaction in work?
4. Do you think this has to be so?
5. Is there some other way in which modern work could be organised so that each person feels that he matters?
6. Does having to work hard mean that you cannot enjoy it?
7. Do you believe that the days of finding satisfaction in work are gone?
8. What do you understand from the story of the hospital?

Let the students ask themselves the following:

1. Are there times when you find yourself cutting corners, taking the easy way out? When?
2. Are there occasions when you finish something rather quickly rather than taking it slowly and carefully so that it is really the best that you can do? When was the last time you did this?
3. What decisions do you need to make so that you can help others to do their best too?

It would help the students if, having written down the specific decisions on these points, they shared them with others. Then their friends and the teacher can help them to keep to the decisions.

ESSAY SUBJECT

Write how you think you can use your talents and gifts for the sake of other people when you leave school.
Note
Some of the students may find it difficult to think what are their own gifts and talents. We suggest that the teacher encourages their friends to tell them what they think. Then they will all be equipped to do the exercise suggested above.

RESOURCE MATERIAL

A LITTLE THING TO SAVE A MILLION MEN

Ross dissected mosquito after mosquito, each one of which cost him two or three hours of intense peering through his microscope, until he had done many hundreds. ... He said, "The screws of my microscope were rusted with sweat from my forehead and my hand, and its last remaining eye-piece was cracked."

By August 1897 he had some thirty promising mosquitoes, all bred from larvae and fed on malaria patients. He dissected one after another, until he had come to the last three, but still he had not traced the parasite in the mosquito body. When he looked at the last three insects on the morning of the 20th April, he saw that one had died; then he decided to look at the last but one, although his eyesight was already fatigued. He took the stomach out and searched the remainder of the body and again found nothing. He could scarcely bring himself to look at the numerous cells of the stomach tissue. ... He had done it a thousand times before, without convincing results.

"But," he said, "The Angel of Fate fortunately laid his hand on my head. ..." He looked and looked again. He saw a circular object which could not be one of the cells of the stomach tissue of the mosquito. In it were black granules exactly like those seen in the malaria parasite. If these were the malaria granules, then they had got into the walls of the mosquito's stomach. He laughed and shouted for his assistant, but he had gone for his siesta. ...

He made careful notes and drawings, went home for tea and slept soundly for an hour. He awoke ... and it occurred to him that if the cells he had seen were indeed a stage of the developing parasite, those in his last remaining mosquito should have grown during the night. On the next morning he arrived at the hospital in intense excitement. He examined his last specimen with a shaking hand. There indeed were the peculiar cells and they were much bigger!

The basic problem was solved at last. ... On the same evening he scribbled:

This day designing God
Hath put into my hand
A wondrous thing. And God
Be praised. At his command
I have found thy secret deeds,
O million-murdering Death.[1]

[1] Adapted from *Readings for the Senior Assembly* edited by D. M. Prescott, Blandford Press.

Change—a way of life

AIMS

To discover the how, when and why of change and to make it the normal way of living for us all. (The teacher's own experience will be most valuable in this topic.)

DEVELOPMENT

By now, if you have been honestly making the experiments suggested in the previous topics, you will have found that things have changed in and around you.

Give time for the students to give examples of how this has happened and what the effects have been. The teacher should also contribute any changes he has experienced or noticed.

Accepting and initiating change is the normal way to live. In nature change is normal.

Change brings growth and development.

What happens in nature when animals have not adapted to their changing conditions? Here is a picture of one of them.

Where do you find these animals today? (Only in museums)
How does this apply to us today?

DISCUSSION

Divide the class into small groups to discuss: "Men have become technological giants, but have remained moral and spiritual dwarfs." Peter Howard.

The following points may help the discussion:

1. Man has adapted to new technological development. Examine the advances made in space science, engineering, medicine etc.
2. In what ways have we remained "moral and spiritual dwarfs"? Do you think that the man who could press the button to start a nuclear war today is a more responsible, less greedy and less selfish person than the man who used the bow and arrow centuries ago?
3. Is the present generation —
   a) less prejudiced
   b) less hate-filled
   c) less power-seeking
   d) more loving
   e) more ready to see the other person's point of view than in past generations?

At this point in history the world is in danger if we do not learn how to deal with the forces inside us which decide our actions. We have discovered devastating power which can be used for the good of mankind or to destroy it. It is more important than ever that man learns to live in the most responsible way that he knows.

Discuss the following statement: "To expect a change in human nature may be an act of faith. But to expect a change in human society without a change in human nature, is an act of lunacy."

WHY DO WE CHANGE AND HOW?

Let the students give their own suggestions, then ask them the following:

1. If you are a very untidy person and someone you respect is coming to see you, what do you do?
2. If you like your teacher very much and you do badly in your exams one term, what will you do in the next?
3. If you have been unkind to someone and later that day you hear that he/she has had a serious accident and is in hospital, what would you do?

Examine these questions closely and their answers. In each case, you have probably decided to change in some way. What has made you change?

Has it been for your own sake or for the sake of someone else? If you have decided not to change, why is that?

Think of the last time that you deliberately decided to change your way of doing things, or your attitude towards someone else. What was the result?

EXPERIMENT

Here is an experiment[1] which has been tried and found successful by thousands of people all over the world. You can try it out for yourself and see how it works. However, like every other experiment, you must follow it step by step and record things honestly.

Materials

Four sheets of paper and one pencil, pen or ball-point.

[1] Make enough copies of this experiment, so that each student can try it out at home.

Method

1. Write one of these headings on each sheet of paper:
   ABSOLUTE HONESTY, ABSOLUTE PURITY, ABSOLUTE UNSELFISH-
   NESS, ABSOLUTE LOVE.
2. Look back on your life and see how it compares with each
   of these standards in turn.
3. Sit silently and listen to the deepest thoughts in your heart.
4. Write down, under each standard in turn, the places where
   you have not lived up to it. (Some people have needed more
   than one sheet of paper for each standard!)
5. Read through what you have written. This is the sort of
   person you have been.
6. Decide what you are going to do about each point. Put
   right all the things which need to be put right. If you need
   to make apologies, do so.
7. Start to live differently in the future and ask God's power
   to help you do it.

Proof

The quality of your life from now onwards and the reaction
to this of your family and friends.
At the next lesson ask how many of the students have conducted
this experiment. It would be excellent if some of them would
share with the class any experiences they had in doing it.
However, their findings should be their own to tell or not as
they wish. The teacher will realise that this is an important
experiment which will take determination and courage to carry
out. It is much more likely that the students will take the
plunge if the teacher has done so and can vouch for its
effectiveness.

HOW OFTEN DO WE NEED TO CHANGE?

The answer to this is, "All the time". Just because we had a
bath yesterday doesn't mean that we don't have to have another
for the next month!
    "Change is not a terminus at which you arrive. It is a
junction where your real journey in life begins." Discuss.
    Ask the students to write down the following questions,
think about them and then write the answers:
1. What sort of person does God want me to be?

2. What things in my character must I develop to become this sort of person?
3. What am I meant to do with my life? What is the next immediate step in this?

Some of the students may like to read out what they have written. Their friends will be able to help them to see the parts of their character on which they should build so that they can continue growing into the person they are meant to be.

A WAY OF LIFE

When man listens, God speaks.
When man obeys, God acts.
When men change, nations change.

Take time every day from now on to listen to that voice in your heart so that you can find out your part in God's plan for the world.

A NEW WORLD ORDER BUILT ON FIRM FOUNDATIONS

"Big doors swing on little hinges"— the story of what happened in the slums of Rio de Janeiro in Brazil. See under "Resource Material".

Students have often found it very useful to meet before school regularly to share the thoughts they have had in their times of listening to the Inner Voice. By doing this with their friends a strategy has emerged which has helped to bring change in their schools, colleges and in their homes and communities. Perhaps the students in your class would like to do this so that their change begins to be mobilized to help others.

RESOURCE MATERIAL

BIG DOORS SWING ON LITTLE HINGES

*This is a story from the shanty towns of Rio de Janeiro
in Brazil.*

Many people came into the big city of Rio from the poorer
areas of the country looking for work. On arrival they found
that there was nowhere for them to live, as the rents were far
too high. In desperation they ended up building illegal shacks
on unoccupied land. Little by little there grew up communities
of these shacks, perched over stagnant swamps, clinging to steep
slopes, crowded in narrow twisting alleys with no water, no
electricity, no drainage and no security.

Hundreds of thousands of people lived in these dwellings
or 'favelas' as they are called in Brazil. Conditions were so awful
that out of every 1,000 babies born, 450 of them would die
during their first year. It was the dream of every mother to
get her children out of these huts. However, there was little
hope of this or even of things getting better where they were.

At every election time these people were promised water,
electricity and other improvements in exchange for their votes.
Once elections were over, these promises were forgotten. Yet,
in spite of these conditions, there was a great community
spirit and families would help others who were even less
fortunate than themselves.

Euclides da Silva lived in one of these favelas. He soon
realised that if he wanted anything done, then he would have
to do it himself. He found out that some favelas had created
their own associations and through their elected presidents had
been able to have direct contact with the government. Thanks
to this initiative they had been able to secure certain improvements for their favelas.

So Euclides began to take initiative and set up an association in his area. As the president of the association, he managed
to get a concession to install electricity. "At first," he said, "I
was genuinely concerned with the welfare of the community,
but soon I realised that my position could bring me considerable
personal advantages." So he bought the electricity from the
company at four cruzeiros a kilowatt and sold it to the people
for eleven cruzeiros. "I pocketed the difference."

Then he heard that his bitter political rival, Amfilofilo, had got the rights to distribute electricity in another part of the favela. Euclides was furious. He wanted to be the only boss. Four times he tried to kill Amfilofilo, but without success. "My life was violence, corruption and womanising," he says. His wife and family were most unhappy. Violence and immorality were rampant in the favela.

One day a film was shown in Euclides' favela. It told a true story of how gang warfare and corruption had been dealt with in the port of Rio. Some of the dockers who had taken this action came with the film. "After the film," says Euclides, "I stayed talking with the dockers and their friends. They told us about absolute standards of honesty, purity, unselfishness and love and the difference it had made in their lives when they began to live by them. They had put right things which were wrong."

All this and much else that he heard made Euclides take an honest look at his life. "I realised I had a struggle within myself — a fight between my greed and ambition and what God wanted from me. I knew I had to clean up my life." He began by asking forgiveness from his wife and telling her of the things he had done behind her back. Then he decided to write to Amfilofilo. "It was stupid for us to be enemies when he also wanted to improve conditions."

However, it wasn't easy to do. He tore up the first three letters which he wrote and finally sent the fourth. Amfilofilo came round to his house and they made friends with each other. Then Euclides decided that he must publicly admit his dishonesty about the electricity charges and decide to charge only five cruzeiros a unit in the future. He also handed in his resignation as president of the association. However, he was re-elected as people felt that now they could trust him.

In favela after favela, Euclides and the dockers told their experiences. Another favela leader said, "I suddenly saw that we favelados were not just one million problems but two million hands to solve those problems." Many other favelas started associations and began to have direct contact with the government.

As a result of these campaigns, the state authorities launched a re-housing programme and created the Company for Popular Housing. Its aim was to build flats and small houses for the favela dwellers which could be sold on a twenty-year credit. The company consulted Euclides and other favela leaders about its plans. The company president said, "The change in the attitudes of the favela leaders made this collaboration very fruitful. We were able to prepare people for their surroundings."

So a dream started to become a reality. Dignity returned and with it new hope was brought to people's faces. There are still many people yet to re-house, including Euclides himself. However, Euclides and his friends are still concerned for the families who have moved to the new, brick-built homes. They fight that the spirit of community born in the hell of the old poverty should spread to the new conditions and from there to the whole world.

Changing difficult people

AIMS

To help the students to find the most effective way of dealing with the people they find difficult. To see how the art of changing people could affect the situation in the world.

DEVELOPMENT

Ask the students to write down the names of all the people they would like to see different and why.
Ask the class:

1. Have you ever tried to change someone? Why did you do it? How did you do it?
2. Have you tried to change things in yourself? What was the result?
3. Is there any connection between questions 1 and 2? If so, what is it?
4. Does it work if we tell people where they are wrong and we are right, and where they need to change? How do you feel when people do this to you?

Note:

It is important that the teacher helps the students to get to the root of why they want to see others different. Very often we want people to change in order to make life easier for us. If this is our motive — an entirely selfish one — we will never be successful. However, if we want people to change for their own sakes, then God will show us how we can help it to happen.

Let the class study the following story:

Everyone considered Victor a very difficult boy. He was a complete rebel and never did anything he was told. At the school camp, high up in the Himalayas, his favourite trick was to pull out all the tent pegs, so that the tent collapsed on the people inside. He never went to any of the camp meetings. The masters in charge wanted to send him back home.

Before doing this, the principal decided to talk to a friend of his, Dr Buchman, who was visiting the camp. Dr Buchman asked if the principal had talked with the boy. "No," he replied. "But we've talked *about* him. Will you talk to him?"

Buchman agreed and the principal said that he would have Victor there at 10.20 in the morning. Victor didn't turn up. Another date was fixed for 2.30. Still he did not appear. That night there was a beautiful full moon. Victor had promised again to come and see Buchman, but instead he was off rowing on the canal. "Who would blame Victor for staying away?" said Buchman.

The next morning the principal rushed into Buchman's room saying, "I've got Victor. Come at once." Dr Buchman went out to a small hill where Victor and another boy were playing. They were twirling bamboo canes around their heads like a drum-major at the head of a band.

Buchman went up to Victor and said, "You do that well. I wish I could do it."

Victor, instead of running away as he usually did, replied, "Well, try it." Dr Buchman tried and failed, which delighted Victor. Then Buchman sat down and said to Victor, "I once went to a camp and hated it."

"Were you like that? I'm like that too." He began to tell Buchman about himself — the things he had done and how he had made a nuisance of himself. He said, "There is something wrong inside me. That's all that can be said about it."

Buchman talked with him. Finally Victor said, "I'm sorry."

"How sorry?" said Buchman. "Do you know what remorse is?"

Victor said, "Yes I know. It is being sorry and then going ahead and doing it again."

"That's not much good," said Buchman.

"No," replied Victor. "What I need is repentance. That means being sorry enough to quit."

Then Dr Buchman talked to Victor about sin with the big "I" as its middle letter. He said that sin is anything that comes between you and God or between you and the other person. He told Victor how he had given himself to God. Victor said, "I would like to do that." With Buchman he then prayed, "Lord, manage me for I can't manage myself."

Victor said later, "It's as if a lot of old luggage that was no good has rolled away. I must go and tell my friends what happened." Months later Buchman visited the school and met many of Victor's fellow students who had been changed through talking with him.

Write down the answers to the following questions:

1. What sort of boy was Victor?
2. The principal was going to send Victor home. Had he tried talking with him first? What had he done?
3. What was Dr Buchman's reaction when Victor did not keep any of the appointments?
4. What two things that Dr Buchman did won Victor's interest?
5. When Victor felt he could trust Buchman, what did he do?
6. What were Victor's definitions of "remorse" and "repentance"?
7. What did Buchman say about sin?
8. What did Victor decide to do after his talk?
9. What did Victor feel like after this decision?
10. What did Victor do in the future?

Study carefully the answers to these questions.

Write down why you think Dr Buchman was able to help Victor to change.

Have you ever tried to do what Dr Buchman did for Victor?

Have you ever made the same decision as Victor made?

What connection do these two things have?

Look back at the names of the people you wrote down at the beginning of this project. What will you do about them?

DISCUSSION TOPIC

"Cabinets to rule well must change people"— Dr Buchman. Do you think this statement is true? Give your reasons. If cabinets did this, how would it affect the situation in the world today?

Here is a story which tells how a class managed to change their teacher. It is told by the teacher herself.

I was a teacher in a high school. The girls in my class were about thirteen years of age. One Monday two of the class came to me and said, "Please will you inspect our desks today?" In this school, the students kept their books, pencils, ink and so on in their desks, only taking home the things they needed for their homework. They hated my habit of inspecting the desks for tidiness, so this request surprised me very much indeed. I thought to myself, "They must have made a special effort today, so I'll do as they ask." That evening, after they had all gone home, I did check their desks and found, as I expected, each one clean and tidy.

On Tuesday I decided to take them by surprise and do another inspection that evening. Again every desk was perfect. I was most impressed. I inspected the desks each day that week with the same result. I was extremely puzzled and a little suspicious by this time!

However, on the next Monday all was explained. At lunch time, the same two girls came to me and said, with great respect, "Please may we help you to tidy *your* desk."

I asked them how they got the co-operation of the whole class in keeping their desks tidy for so long and they explained. "Last week a visitor came to our classroom. Some of us felt very ashamed of your untidy desk. Then when we talked about it afterwards, we realised that ours were just as bad, but they could not be seen. So we collected the whole class together in the playground and asked them to keep their desks absolutely tidy for a week so that we could help you to be tidy."

During the previous weeks I had been explaining to them that if they wanted to help anyone else to change, they had to start with themselves. They had applied this philosophy in practice and had helped me to see my fault in a very effective way. I have always been very grateful for the lesson they taught me and it has helped me ever since.

Music

Water for a thirsty land

Words and Music by
KATHLEEN JOHNSON

Moderate, with a lilt

Wa — ter for a thir-sty land, Cool wa-ter, cool wa-ter, who'll bring wa-ter for a thir-sty land? *Wa-ter for a thir-sty land — *Wa-ter for a thir-sty land. 1. The world is like a de-sert Where the land is parched and dry, And peo-ple burn with a thirst for things That just don't sa-tis-fy. — 2. And mil-lions drink from the rivers of hate That seem so swift and sure, They burn with a might-y pas-sion That can ne-ver bring a cure.

3. There is a stream of water
   That will fill and satisfy,
   It comes to you as you give it away,
   And it never, never runs dry.

4. I've counted all my treasures,
   And the things I long to do,
   I'll gladly give the best I have,
   Till the world has a purpose new.
   [* - * twice in final chorus]

When I point my finger at my neighbour

Arranged by
PENELOPE THWAITES

Words and Music by
CECIL BROADHURST

Rhythmical and not too fast

When I point my fin-ger at my

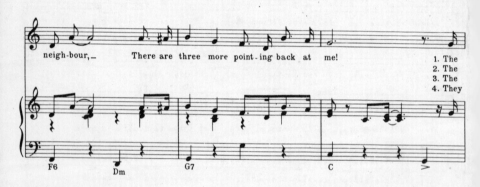

neigh-bour,— There are three more point-ing back at me!

1. The
2. The
3. The
4. They

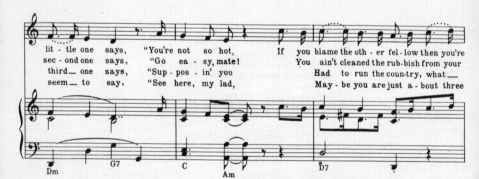

lit - tle one says, "You're not so hot, If you blame the oth - er fel - low then you're
sec - ond one says, "Go ea - sy, mate! You ain't cleaned the rub-bish from your
third— one says, "Sup - pos - in' you Had to run the coun-try, what—
seem— to say, "See here, my lad, May - be you are just a - bout three

God has a plan

Lyric by
ALAN THORNHILL

Music by
GEORGE FRASER

THE WORLD IS TORN WITH STRIFE AND CHAOS THREATENS THE HU-MAN PLANS WE PUT OUR FAITH IN DON'T SUC-CEED WE FOR-GET THAT BOTH IN FAMILIES AND IN NATIONS HUMAN WISDOM FAILS MUST AL-WAYS FAIL ___ OUR DEEPEST NEED. GOD HAS A PLAN YOU HAVE A PART OH EV'RY WO-MAN AND MAN OPEN YOUR HEART, TO THE SIMPLE FACT THAT GOD CAN GUIDE YOU BY THE

Please, Thank you and Sorry

Lyric by
PETER HOWARD

Music by
GEORGE FRASER

Voice

Piano

Andante moderato

1.& 3. Please, thank you and sor - ry—
2. Please, thank you and sor - ry—

Mag - i - cal, mag - i - cal sounds,— Mak - ing peo - ple from pig -
Sim - ple to say,— it's true,— Not so sim - ple or ea -

- gies,— Hum - ans from hors - es and hounds. An
- sy— When you real - ly mean— it too.

Three mag - i - cal phras - es, Help - ing us all to see—
un - fail - ing man - oeu - vre For bring - ing a fight to an

3rd time to Coda

How to stop be-ing the folk that we are_ And be-come what we're meant to be.
end, And a prac-ti-cal tip if you're wanting to turn An en-e-my in - to a

F6   Dm   G7   C   C Cm G   G7

So it's "please", when you want a cake_ And "thanks" for a
friend. It's the same for the young and old,_ The duke and the

C   E   Fdim   F#m   B7   E   Fdim

can - dy, And when you are in the wrong Then "sor - ry" comes in han-dy.
dust-man, The same for the boys and girls, The bish-op and the bus-man.

F#m B7   E   Fdim   F#m   B7   E   Dm7   G7

-come what we're meant to be._____

CODA.

G7   G7   C   Bb   C

Oh, you don't love God if you don't love your neighbour

152

Lyric by SULLIVAN

Music by COLEY

2. Now I know a fellow who said "Hallelujiah
   God has entered my whole life"
   But either he was fooling or he had no memory
   'Cos at home he was always fighting with his wife.

   CHORUS

3. There's a God Almighty and we've got to love Him
   If we want salvation and a home on high,
   But if you say you love Him and you hate your neighbour
   Then you don't have religion, you just told a lie!

   CHORUS

Bibliography

GENERAL

*From India with Hope** Michael Henderson, Grosvenor Books
(A source of many storiese of change coming in people and situations in
    India)
*Handbook of Hope,** ed. Padmini Kirtane, Himmat Publications
*Black and White Book,** Cook and Lean, Blandford
*Art of Remaking Men,** Paul Campbell, Himmat Publications
(This book covers many of the points raised in the Basic Course —
    Topics I to X)
*Senior Teacher's Assembly Book; Readings for the Senior Assembly;
    More Readings for the Senior Assembly,* Dorothy Prescott, Blandford
(These three books have more stories which could be used in addition
    to those given in the course)
Selected writings of Mahatma Gandhi, Ronald Duncan, Faber & Faber
Himmat newsweekly
(Can provide much useful material for discussion and also information)

TOPIC I

Only One Earth, Ward & Dubos, Pelican
The Doomsday Book, C. R. Taylor, Thames & Hudson
Future Shock, Alvin Toffler, Bantam
Hidden Persuaders, Vance Packard, Pelican

TOPIC II

Small is Beautiful, E. F. Schumacher, Abacus
The Muslim Mind, C. Waddy, Longmans
A Short Life of Swami Vivekananda, Swami Pavitrananda, Advaita
    Ashram, Mayavati, Almora
Bal Gangadhar Tilak (A study), D. P. Karmarkar, Popular Prakashan
Vision & Works of Sri Aurobindo, K. D. Sethna, Popular Prakashan
J. N. Tata (A Chronicle of his life), F. R. Harris, Blackie & Son (India)

Rabindranath Tagore, Amar Chitra Katha No. 136, India Book House
    Education Trust
Subhas Chandra Bose, Amar Chitra Katha No. 77, India Book House
    Education Trust
Vivekananda, Amar Chitra Katha No. 146, India Book House Education
    Trust

TOPIC III

Cancer Ward, A. Solzhenitsyn, Fontana
The First Circle, A. Solzhenitsyn, Fontana
The Discovery of India, Jawaharlal Nehru, Asia Publishing House

TOPIC V

My Experiments with Truth, Mohandas Gandhi, Navajivan

TOPIC VIA

My Experiments with Truth, Mohandas Gandhi, Navajivan
The Cult of Softness, Lunn and Lean, Blandford
The New Morality, Lunn and Lean, Blandford
(These two books give other references)

TOPIC VIIIA

My Land and My People, Dalai Lama, Panther
The Life of Mahatma Gandhi, Louis Fischer, Bharatiya Vidya Bhavan
Mao Tse Tung — Emperor of the Blue Ants, George Paloczi-Horvath,
    Secker & Warburg
Memoirs of the Viscount Montgomery of Alamein, Fontana/Collins
Vinoba — His Life & Work, Shriman Narayan, Popular Prakashan
Service before Self, Anand Hingorani, Bhavan's Publications

TOPIC VIIIB

The Challenge of World Poverty, Gunnar Myrdal

TOPIC IX

Something Beautiful for God, Malcolm Muggeridge, Fontana/Collins
Strength to Love, Martin Luther King
More than Conquerors, Graham Turner, Hodder & Stoughton

TOPIC X

Escape to Live, E. Howell, Longmans
My Experiments with Truth, Mohandas Gandhi, Navajivan
God's Smuggler, Brother Andrew, Hodder & Stoughton
Geoffery, G. Appleyard, Blandford
Food for the Soul, Anand Hingorani, Bhavan's Publications

TOPIC XI

Great Lives, Wilson College, Popular Prakashan
Dr Zakir Husain, M. Mujeeb, National Book Trust India
The Indomitable Sardar, K. L. Panjabi, Bhavan's Book University
Paramhansa Sri Ramakrishna, R. R. Diwakar, Bhavan's Book University
Ranade — The Prophet of Liberated India, D. G. Karve, Popular
    Prakashan
Buddha, Amar Chitra Katha, India Book House Education Trust
*Guru Gobind Singh; Ashoka; Guru Nanak; Zarathushtra; Mahavir;
    Dr Ambedkar*, Amar Chitra Katha, India Book House Education
    Trust
Brave Men Choose, Garth Lean, Blandford
Dr Ida; Take My Hands, Dorothy Clarke Wilson, Hodder
Florence Nightingale, Cecil Woodham Smith, Constable
Mr Wilberforce M. P., Alan Thornhill, Blandford
The People's Earl, M. St. J. Fancourt, Longmans
*The World My Country** (*The Life of Daw Nyein Tha*) Marjorie
    Proctor, Grosvenor

TOPIC XII

My Life with Martin Luther King, Coretta King, Avon
The Muslim Mind, C. Waddy, Longmans
*Playing to Win,** Conrad Hunte, Himmat Publications
*Out of the Evil Night,** Leif Hovelsen, Blandford

TOPIC XIII

*A New World for my Grandchildren**, Charlotte van Beuningen,
    Himmat Publications
Reach for the Sky, Douglas Bader, Collins
Diary of Anne Frank, Pan
The Small Woman, Alan Burgess, Evans
Alone, Richard E. Byrd, Putnam
*God's Hand in History** — series, Mary Wilson, Blandford
Sister Nivedita, Basudha Chakravarty, National Book Trust India
Harishchandra, Amar Chitra Katha, India Book House Education
    Trust
Prahlad, Amar Chitra Katha, India Book House Education Trust

TOPIC XIV

Kinship and Marriage, Norah Cook, Blandford Social Studies
We Nehrus, Krishna Nehru Hutheesing, Pearl
*Rebirth of a Nation,** Garth Lean, Blandford
The Web of Indian Life, S. Minechita

TOPIC XV

Madam Curie, Eve Curie, Pocket Books
Six Great Doctors, J. G. Crowther, Hamish Hamilton

Stories from Bapu's Life, Umashanker Joshi, National Book Trust India
What life has taught me, several contributors, Bhavan's Book University
Kabir, Amar Chitra Katha, India Book House Education Trust

TOPIC XVII

*Frank Buchman's Secret,** Peter Howard, Heinemann
*Teenagers in Revolt,** P. V. Abraham, Himmat

All enquires about the books marked* to:
Grosvenor Books, 54 Lyford Road, London SW18 3JJ.

Also available from Moral Re-Armament at:
21 Dorcas Street, South Melbourne, Victoria 3205, Australia.
387 Cote St. Catherine Road, Montreal, P.Q. H2V 2B5, Canada.
P.O. Box 1874, 33 Elefth Venizelos Street, Nicosia, Cyprus.
Flat A-2, 9th Floor, 2 Oaklands Path, Hong Kong.
Box 20035, Nairobi, Kenya.
Casa Vilhena, Sacred Heart Avenue, St. Julius, Malta, GC.
P.O. Box 1834, Wellington, New Zealand.
Box 2102, Lagos, Nigeria.
Box 5413, Boroko, Papua New Guinea.
Box 10144, Johannesburg, South Africa.
Mountain House, CH 1824 Caux, Switzerland.
Suite 702, 124 East 40th Street, New York, NY 10016, USA.
Box 1735, Ndola, Zambia.

Films and audio-visual material

Happy Deathday, Technicolour, 89 minutes
The generation gap explodes in a wealthy family. The rich grandfather, a man of faith, is dying. The atheist son-in-law is a brilliant scientist who is experimenting with frozen animation. Grand-daughter Jetta is a typical girl in a permissive age.
Suitable for Standard X upwards
Topics I, IV

Galloping Horse, colour, 18 minutes
Divided farmer brothers get united. Harijans take responsibility for the education of their people. A new spirit at work among ordinary people.
Topics II, VIIIB, XI

A Nation is Marching, colour, 22 minutes
Rajmohan Gandhi's "March on Wheels" from Cape Comorin to New Delhi when thousands thronged to join his campaign for "a clean, strong and united India".
Topics II, III, V, VIIIA, XVI

Asian Experiment, colour, 23 minutes
Vivid shots of the application of absolute moral standards and the guidance of God in ordinary people from Sri Lanka to Assam.
Topics IV, V, X, XII

Asia's Destiny, colour, 25 minutes
Reconciliation between Chinese and Malay in Malaysia; the inauguration of the state of Meghalaya; trade unionist and businessmen give practical experiences of a new factor at work.
Topics III, VIIIA IX, X, XI, XII, XVII

Give a Dog a Bone, colour musical, 77 minutes
The story of a boy, Mickey Merry, his dog Ringo and Mr Space, a visitor from another planet, their enemy King Rat who changes people

into animals, and their victorious battle for good against evil.
Topics VIB, VII, X, XVII

Mr Brown Comes Down the Hill, black and white, 80 minutes
Three people go up a hill to find God. They invite Mr Brown, whom
they meet there, to come down and face the modern world.
Suitable for Standard X upwards.
Topics IX, X, XIII

Voice of the Hurricane, Technicolour, 80 minutes
Filmed in Africa, the action centres on a settler's farm where a visiting
Member of Parliament is caught up in a violent nationalist uprising.
Suitable for Standard IX upwards.
Topics IX, X, XII

A Man for All People, colour 30 minutes
The life of Dr William Nkomo of South Africa, the founder of the
African National Youth Congress. The story of a man who found a cure
to hate amidst every opportunity to harbour bitterness.
Topics IX, XI, XII, XIII

Build on Solid Ground, colour slides with a taped commentary
The story of the favelas of Brazil.
Topic XVI

All enquiries about these films to:
12, Palace Street, London SW1.

Also to Moral Re-Armament at:
21 Dorcas Street, South Melbourne, Victoria 3205, Australia.
387 Cote St. Catherine Road, Montreal, P.Q. H2V 2B5, Canada.
P.O. Box 1874, 33 Elefth Venizelos Street, Nicosia, Cyprus.
Flat A-2, 9th Floor, 2 Oaklands Path, Hong Kong.
Box 20035, Nairobi, Kenya.
Casa Vilhena, Sacred Heart Avenue, St. Julius, Malta, GC.
P.O. Box 1834, Wellington, New Zealand.
Box 2102, Lagos, Nigeria.
Box 5413, Boroko, Papua New Guinea.
Box 10144, Johannesburg, South Africa.
Mountain House, CH 1824 Caux, Switzerland.
Suite 702, 124 East 40th Street, New York, NY 10016, USA.
Box 1735, Ndola, Zambia.

Index